Robert Harbinson was born in Belfast in 1928 and he was educated there and in Enniskillen, Co. Fermanagh. He worked for a short time as a cabin boy on a dredger in Belfast Lough, then started training as a medical missionary. He left Belfast in 1944 to study theology at the South Wales Bible College and he went on to teach in north Devon, Canada and Venezuela. He took up diamond prospecting in Canada and South America and his hunting and trapping with the Blackfoot and Stony Indians began a long interest in American Indians who feature in his many travel books which were published in the 1960s under the name of Robin Bryans.

In more recent years he has become involved in music, concentrating on his work as an opera librettist from his London home/music studio.

The Protégé is the last volume of his four-part autobiography which begins with *No Surrender* and continues with *Song of Erne* and *Up Spake the Cabin Boy*. In addition to these and his travel books he has also published *Tattoo Lily and Other Ulster Stories*, the novel *Lucio*, and his collection of poems *Songs Out of Oriel*.

D0543810

The Protégé

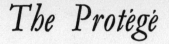

ROBERT HARBINSON

THE
BLACKSTAFF
PRESS
BELFAST AND ST PAUL, MINNESOTA

First published in 1963 by
Faber and Faber Limited
This Blackstaff Press edition is a photolithographic facsimile
of the first edition printed by Latimer Trend & Company Limited

This edition published in 1988 by
The Blackstaff Press Limited
3 Galway Park, Dundonald, Belfast BT16 0AN, Northern Ireland
and
Box 5026, 2115 Summit Avenue, St Paul, Minnesota 55105, USA
with the assistance of
The Arts Council of Northern Ireland

Printed by The Guernsey Press Company Limited

British Library Cataloguing in Publication Data
Harbinson, Robert, 1928–
The protégé.
1. Northern Ireland. Harbinson, Robert, 1928–
I. Title
941.6082'2'0924
ISBN 0-85640-413-6

Nous n'irons plus aux bois, les
lauriers sont coupés.

THÉODORE DE BANVILLE

Contents

Apostrophe to the Reader

❧❦❧

The events related in this, the fourth part of my auto-biography, happened in comparatively modern times. Pre-1939 war poverty is now far behind and I bring the story up to 1949, a year of disgrace rather than grace for me.

When I left Ireland, I was determined to get on in life and to use any means which came my way. The several rungs of the evangelical ladder proved to be as good as any. With no scruples and little conscience I began to climb it.

This is my story, this is my song. . . .

However, I want to make it plain that I met many fine people amongst those who befriended me and promoted my interests. Though I am no longer of evangelical persuasion, much of my friends' character with its cleanliness and godliness has rubbed off on to me. I would not like to offend these people by this book or cause pain to their surviving relatives, and I have decided to be discreet by changing names of people and places where offence might be taken. But certain well-known figures inevitably feature in this book of climbing. Both in life and after they were quite incapable of disguise, and so they appear on my canvas as large as my brush will paint them.

CHAPTER I

Pomegranates

❦❦❦

I have to admit that it was Tinkerbell, and not the Lord, who swept me to the heights of success. At the time, of course, I tended to agree with the 'praying partners' I had just left behind in Ireland. They held the unshakable view that none other than the Lord was leading me on every step of the journey. Appearances could not help but create this impression. Had I not risen from lowly service in the galley of a mud dredger in Belfast Lough to the glory of being the student in Room Number One of the Beulah Bible Academy? And had not several extraordinary stumbling blocks miraculously become stepping-stones? There was a war on, as people used to say in those days. Also, I was only sixteen. Yet I had crossed the Water, prohibitions on travel being rolled aside as the Red Sea once was. Who could doubt but that these things were the Lord's doing?

So there I was, of all people, and, of all places, in Wales, walking down a long hill on the last lap of my journey from Ireland. Perhaps on that Saturday afternoon I mistook my adolescent thrill in new adventure for divine inspiration. At any rate, as I walked with a swing down that hill, I was conscious that extraordinary events had overtaken the boy from Belfast's back streets, and the evacuee from the Ulster countryside, and the young man who had tried his hand at many trades in Belfast. Instead of being a greasy shipyard apprentice as once intended, I had become a smart young chap in a collar. Not so much as a speck dirtied his hands.

9

Feeling pleased, excited and smug, I saw Tinkerbell. She was cropping grass on a stretch of waste land between the police station and the Navvy Mission. I did not stop. There was no time just then for irrelevancies. I had to find the Beulah Bible Academy. This was easy and a few minutes after leaving Tinkerbell, who had not the faintest idea who I was, people took me in who had a very clear idea concerning my identity. To them, I was the Miracle Boy.

I trailed miracles behind me like star dust. *The Times* on the Principal's table, for instance, told how the ban on travel from Northern Ireland, imposed because of the impending invasion, might be lifted the following week, but only on cargo shipping. The bulletin made no mention of when passenger services would be allowed to start again, and only then for those with permits and passes. How was it, then, that the Miracle Boy had been able to travel from Ireland? This was one of the miracles. He was carried by grace alone from the horrors of Catholic Ireland into the bosom of the Beulah Bible Academy.

What better proof of the Lord's blessing on its work of training ministers and missionaries could the Academy desire?

I hung my mantle of miracles on the hat-stand in the hall, along with my rolled umbrella and I went into the long, chill corridors of the Academy. My arrival created quite a stir, or as much of a stir as could be made in a vast, empty building. Because the summer vacation had only just started, all the other students were away. Most of them were busy evangelizing in the Welsh valleys. But the staff made up for the lack of quantity by the quality of their welcome. In spite of their own ardent praying, they had not really believed that I would beat the travel ban. And now, there I was, actually standing in the sombre rooms of the Bible Academy.

The Lord's hand indeed! With some justification now the Academy could keep its front door firmly shut in the faces of billeting officers still desperate for war-time accommodation. Cardiff's Lord Mayor himself might knock in vain upon that door for the latest evacuees escaping the V-2 bombs on London. Clearly, the Lord's blessing rested over the house and its work, and it was only right that it should be preserved solely for that work.

Room Number One, the Academy's equivalent of the Oliver Messel suite at the Dorchester, was given to me because I was the Miracle Boy. But Spartan was the word and Spartan clearly the action in the Academy. Ugliness was next to godliness. Cleanliness and virtue were synonymous. The ugliness perhaps could be excused, for there was little made by man in South Wales which was not ugly. I found the cleanliness, however, more difficult to bear with. It consisted of an enamel jug in an enamel bowl standing on a washstand with an enamel slop-bucket underneath.

This jug, identical with all its fellows in all the other rooms, had to be filled daily from the taps in the Academy's one bathroom on the way back from emptying slops. This meant a considerable journey along devious passages and staircases. Even if the water was hot at the source, it was tepid by the time the student carried it to the bedroom, and certainly cold and sometimes frozen by the time he used it next morning. The rigours of winter in no way mitigated this ritual. Naturally, this Spartan behaviour made the incubation of sinful thoughts rather difficult. The embryo ministers and missionaries were much too busy trying to survive than to bother with such luxuries as sin.

Another advantage of the ugliness and the cleanliness was that future missionaries would find the hardships of the field a comparative relief. Tropical heat, flies and filth would be a welcome change. A hammock in a bamboo hut would hardly be more uncomfortable than the horsehair pallet laid unseductively on the unyielding springs of the Academy's iron bedsteads.

In spite of its barrenness, the fact that Room Number One was to be my very own filled me with a sense of achievement. Sophisticated taste was at that time still foreign to me. As far as I was concerned, I had arrived. The going through the training, the taking of examinations, the interviews with missionary councils, appeared as mere, and perhaps even irritating, details. In my own mind I was on the threshold of my life's work as a missionary.

As though to underline the life-work, a map of the world had been pasted on the bedroom wall, providing simultaneously the room's principal décor. This God's-eye-view of the world greeted each student as he woke in the morning. His thoughts could but fly out to the waiting vineyards spread Mercatorwise before him.

So many hesitations and falterings, so many doubting hours and false starts had dogged the two years I spent in Belfast after my return from being an evacuee in the country. Sometimes it had seemed that my whole life would be nothing but a rudderless drift on a sea of uncertainty. And now I was installed as a student with the future clear and shining before me. Nothing could ever go wrong any more.

And this was clearly a miracle, a private miracle for me alone. No wonder I saw the Lord's fingerprints everywhere. Because on that July afternoon, the grass-cropping Tinkerbell had not yet entered my life, so it was natural for me to ascribe my success to the Almighty. There could not be a more appropriate expressing of thanks than by plunging immediately into a frenzy of praying and preaching. The war had taken off many of the older men so that local churches and mission halls had to rely on student labour in the pulpit and platform. Since the other Academy students were scattered like sheep in shepherds' clothing among the Welsh valleys, ample opportunity existed for me to do my stuff in the nearby places of worship.

Within twenty-four hours of installing myself in Room Number One I had spoken at the Sailors' Rest and in the big sanatorium out at Sully. According to the best evangelical tradition, in which I was well versed, my talks had to be of the 'testimony' kind, with a heavy personal bias. Presumably the psychological conditions which drive some people to talk of their operations, similarly drive others to talk of their soul's salvation, using the advertiser's before-and-after technique. I took my text from the Book of Numbers, chapter eleven, verse twenty—*Why came we forth out of Egypt?*

Goodness knows, now, why. But then it all had a high-sounding purpose. That phrase from holy scripture was to become my signature tune in the scores of my sermons. The other first year students, I discovered, served up their instant Gospel in the form of John iii, 16. But I liked my Numbers with its flavour of the exotic. Egypt! Well, there was something for a young missionary. Who knew but that I might go a-missioning in Egypt myself. And I already felt some kinship with the land of the Pharoahs. The Egypt General Mission had been founded by seven young men from my native Belfast. One of them was a lawyer. The head of the firm with which he was a partner had been led by the Lord to be instrumental in getting me aboard the troopship.

Moreover, by using the Numbers text, the flesh-pots I had left behind in Ulster (much less interesting in fact than the present need for platform-sensation would allow) could easily be compared with the cucumbers and melons of Egypt. And the irresistible attraction of those ancient leeks and garlic could be likened to the smoking and swearing of 'unsaved' days. I must have developed quite a way of verbally handling the oriental garden produce because many years afterwards an old lady came up to me on Paddington Station and asked wasn't I the young man with the pomegranates?

Pomegranates indeed! The Academy students enjoyed little luxury. And worse still, most of them had no sense of luxury either, and those that did, regarded it as sinful or at best, highly suspect. Yet in a curious way they indulged themselves gluttonously on prayers and sermons of inordinate length and unseemly emotion.

Nothing of my own first sermon at Sully sanatorium comes back now except the fright given me by Sister Winifred. Sanatoria held no terrors for me, at least no unknown terrors. The first twelve years of my life had been punctuated by weekly visits to tuberculosis clinics and long 'lie-ins' in Belfast hospitals. When the threat of German bombs sent thousands of Belfast children, including me, scurrying into the idyllic but unknown West Ulster countryside, there was not much I did

13

not know about sanatoria. And if, when I became a preacher later, I had an obsession with death perhaps it was because death had once had an obsession with me, as with tubercular children. Death never let us alone, so that we became blasé about it. Instinctively we asked, 'What happens *after*wards?' None of us believed that people, we ourselves, actually *died*. And interest in such matters was coldly technical like wanting to know how motor-bikes worked.

So although I was bewildered and confused a lot of the time by the multitude of theories offered by various sects, I never once doubted that religion itself was important. Consequently, with no qualms or doubts and with no sense of incongruity, I stood in front of my audience at Sully sanatorium and spoke to the doomed and the desperate about eternal life. I had to use a microphone because the patients too ill to get up listened to me through earphones in bed. The microphone put me off. Nor was I too comfortable knowing that many of my listeners were invisible to me. However, when I looked around the main hall and saw the men and women wrapped in red blankets and brown check dressing-gowns, I knew that the plucked brand was expected to glow. I glowed as best as I knew how. And it was when I stopped that Sister Winifred frightened me.

A salvo of praise pierced my ear. The blast of it nearly knocked me off the platform. I knew that Sister Winifred was the Matron of our Bible Academy. But I did not know that she was an ex-heroine of the evangelical movement, a kind of Marlene Dietrich of the mission halls, whose voice had brought her fame without fortune. It would have been not only harsh but incorrect to have described Sister Winifred as trying to stage a come-back. She had never been off the stage since the golden days of long ago described in one obituary which revealed her as being 'caught in the flame of the 1904–5 Revival'.

I was certainly caught by her 'gift of song', a gift from which the tunefulness had long since departed leaving not a rack behind except her justly celebrated volume. Luckily, Sister Winifred was possessed of other less noisy gifts, notably a flair for organization. She owed her position as Matron of the

Academy to this and also her able handling of the shop and Bible depot attached to the Academy.

It was her capacity in this direction rather than her singing which led me on. And Sister Winifred's manifold tasks connected with books brought me a tiny splinter of fame which was to lead to the biggest of changes in my life so far. None of this would have happened had not Tinkerbell been innocently grazing on the waste lot as I arrived at the Academy from Ireland. Tinkerbell would have remained to blush unseen in the desert of her waste lot if there had been no Convention Week and no Sister Winifred who fed the Convention with books.

Sister Winifred's business year with Bibles was a trickle, but Convention Week was a flood. The Academy's Bible shop not only supplied the Convention itself with holy and approved literature but also the special bookstalls set up in connection with the Convention in the town's churches. Sister Winifred proved herself an able economist regarding the laws of supply and demand.

In spite of the war and the ascetic life it forced upon believers and unbelievers alike, there was no shortage of Bibles and other godly books. The Bibles abounded in a score of languages. The other, more modern, writings for which a lesser degree of inspiration was claimed, were in such multiplicity that a shortage of any one particular publication could always be adequately compensated by some other evangelical work. The war, however, did impose one problem on Sister Winifred. Heavy boxes full of books could not be delivered without transport, and this was difficult to arrange.

My first week-end in the Bible Academy went quickly by. Before I had time to reflect on the effect of my sermon at Sully sanatorium, it was Monday morning and the first day of Convention Week. Winifred was a worried sister. Missionaries and Christian Workers already swarmed in the corridors of the student-less Academy, and, so far, no arrangements had been made about book transport. How would she be able to face the distinguished people at the Convention knowing that she had failed in her duty? What, for instance, could she say to one of our famous speakers, the chairman of the Keswick Convention itself, a man who featured as a species of archbishop in our evangelical world? In all the excitement the Miracle Boy from Ireland would be forgotten as reports came in from German and Japanese concentration camps and from South American rain-forests stewing in the cauldron of Roman Catholicism. But would Sister Winifred's failure to organize the book transport be similarly forgotten?

On the Monday morning I was out of bed even before the Spartan hour expected of me, and long before the Convention people were due to arrive. The Academy needed to be prepared, and I soon saw how ineffective the staff were when it came to practical affairs. Two years on Fermanagh farms and two years in various city jobs in Belfast had made me into a useful handyman. So I scurried round the Academy doing a dozen jobs which other people either could not do or took too long to do. I finished well before time, at eight o'clock I was hoisting the flag.

The flag was not in fact a flag as such, but large letters painted on the roof slates advising those who read them that 'God is love'. As with most simplifications of complicated Biblical propostitions, we all understood this statement to be qualified. To members of the Convention, God was, of course, love. But our roof message carried the inevitable corollary, warning sinners that unless they got 'saved' they would pretty soon discover that God was *not* love, especially when they found themselves roasting painfully but eternally combustible in hell. This message with its typical evangelical overtones of divine violence was easily visible from the nearby railway. Sinners on their way to Barry Island, where they would lie profanely half-naked to try and get a tan from the summer sun, could not help but see the roof message.

While I was clambering about on the slates with my pot of paint I had a brain-wave about Sister Winifred's unsolved transport problem. Let the Army Scripture Readers be unco-operative about their wretched van I thought, I would get the hundreds of books to the Convention myself. My vision was of none other than Tinkerbell herself, still contentedly munching on her waste lot. The more I looked down at her from the roof, the more I saw how sleek and fat she had become from years of inactivity. Well, she should cease from that very morning to be lazy. Like the rest of us she should be harnessed to the Lord's service.

Hames and breeching came as easily to me as Psalms and Proverbs. I was probably more thrilled at the prospect of harnessing up a beast and so briefly tasting the idylls of Fermanagh again, than I was with being a servant for the Lord in His great work of the Convention. But whatever the motive, I was down from the God-is-love roof as quick as lightning and away off to the miner's dwelling by the Navvy Mission, to try and find Tinkerbell's owner. The man had no objection to his pony being impressed. Within the hour I had my Bibles and Testaments, my *Streams in the Desert* and *War on the Saints* up behind me on the trap and Tinkerbell in full rein.

We went through the city traffic at a pace which frightened even me—I who once used to take the fieriest of stallions to stud. But with life and limb still more or less together both Tinkerbell and I arrived at the Convention site. And although my chariot of fire was nothing more than a scrap-dealer's spring-trap, and a borrowed one at that, even the President of the Fellowship of Independent Evangelical Churches could not fail to acknowledge us.

Success went to my head. Promise boxes and *Daily Lights* went like hot cakes. The coffers of Sister Winifred's Bible depot began to fill. Ours was a second Keswick, with packed houses at every show. Although my Belfast experience of preaching and preachers had been wide, such pulpit fireworks as I heard now had never dazzled me in all my sixteen years. I believed, quite genuinely, that the Lord was 'very near'.

Feeling rather like the man in the parable who was commended for his profitable work with fine talents, I made myself useful around the Convention. Not only had I arrived from Ireland endowed with the gift of handling horses, but I also had a camera. This made me much sought after for photographing groups. Rolls of film were scarce because of the war. But the chemist shop in Belfast where I once worked saw to it that I was never short of film. By the end of the Convention there were few members who did not know about the young Irish student at the Academy. In any case, I saw personally to it that they did.

But for me, the Convention was really a matter of filling in time. It had already been decided to send me off on our evangelizing mission into the Welsh valleys. Before going, however, I had established myself thoroughly in the Academy, and by a combination of energy and flattery had become a firm favourite with Sister Winifred.

All sorts of ideas occurred to the Academy Matron when she saw me in the pony-trap driving poor Tinkerbell hell for leather and cutting through the traffic like a latter day Boadicea. Perhaps the way I carted those Bibles about from Academy to Convention, from church to chapel, convinced the deaconess that I was indeed the Miracle Boy. At any rate, she determined to extend the scope of the miraculous and to extend it in fact, from colportage to interior decoration, in particular to the re-arrangement of her bedroom furniture.

Would I led a hand? Of course I would. Even when I went upstairs into her sanctum and found that although heaven and earth might well pass away this massive furniture would certainly never do so, I remained willing to sweat. But more than of my physical labours, Sister Winifred was glad of my ideas. Why shut out God's light streaming in the window by such a huge dressing-table? And surely the wardrobe would be better on *this* wall because it was difficult to squeeze past it at the door?

And no sooner had I completed my architectural schemes upstairs than Sister Winifred remembered the Bible Shop window. She made no bones about hating to dress the window. So out came the hideous *crêpe* paper for the making of yellow streamers and red roses. My scissors snipped at borders and cunningly cut Egyptian deserts. Sister Winifred was delighted with the results and for a year afterwards I was window-dresser in chief and eventually adviser to the Matron about her dress.

Having wrought these miracles, I received my reward. Sister Winifred called me by my Christian name. Honour indeed! None of the other students was accorded it, for the deaconess was not only the Academy's Matron but the Principal's all-powerful wife.

So with the hierarchy's blessing I packed a tin trunk with religious literature in English and Welsh and turned my eyes to the hills and particularly to the valleys between them. Within less than a fortnight of arriving in Wales I was going out to the mission field, in the train bound for Monmouthshire. But I had been long enough at the Bible Academy to know that I was expected to sow my pomegranate seeds of witness among the cigarette-smoking sinners in the compartment.

CHAPTER II

Apples of Gold

❧❀❧

I was sixteen years old and all the world seemed beautiful, especially Abergavenny as the train puffed into it in the evening. I had to catch a bus into the inky folds of the hills. Already the Sugar Loaf was no more than a silhouette with obtrusive clarity against the sky. And nightfall was complete by the time I reached the church which was to be my home for the next two months.

I found the Gospel caravan resting under a high hedge in the churchyard. From an open door of the church a stripe of yellow light fell across the neglected grass. The door's hinges groaned when I pushed. An oil lamp showed that I stood in the vestry and that a young man was preparing a supper of rice over a primus stove.

We introduced ourselves with mutual expressions of pleasure at our forthcoming work together in the vineyard. But I think my enthusiasm suffered from my hunger. The train journey and a sharp walk up the valley from the bus stop had given me an appetite which the smell of burning rice sharpened into a pain. Brother Stephen, who waved a wooden spoon as he spoke, wanted full details of my adventures both in and out of the Lord. And before we could dig into the rice there had to be thanksgiving and prayer for my safe arrival at the caravan mission.

Brother Stephen told me how anxious he was to leave soon. He wanted to get under way with preparations for his ordination into the Scottish Church. I learnt also that his fellow-worker, Brother William, was on the eve of departure for Africa. They had not been able to leave their valley outposts, however, until I came to relieve them. Both young men belonged to a band of students who had led a most successful mission among the villages of central Wales. The valleys ran with the joyful Gospel news just as the valley streams sang and rejoiced when swollen with rains from the high ground. The missioners held services on most nights of the week, covering a large district. On the Lord's Day itself each of them had several pulpit engagements. Alongside this continuous occupation of the churches and chapels there went a relentless attack on the unsuspecting populace by open-air witnessing and preaching in the village market-places. No stony hearts were left unturned. The campaigners shouted their message to old and young, native and foreign alike. Children on their summer holidays were glad enough of some fresh distraction and sat in circles singing hymns and listening to doctored Bible stories. Perhaps the most bewildered theologically but the most grateful at a more human level were the Italian prisoners of war. Nobody approached them with such warmth as the brothers in evangelism. And although I am sure the Italians had but very little idea, if any, of what these friendly people were on about, they were doubtless grateful for this touch of colour in the drab landscape of captivity.

For more than a year in Ireland I had been accustomed to the exaggerated behaviour of evangelical extremists. And this preaching rolled like so much water off this duck's back. But even so, I was not quite prepared for the tenacity of my brother evangelists in the Welsh valleys. With a fierce courage quite disproportionate to the results produced, they defied world, flesh and devil, king and country. There was practically nothing to which they did not object, and almost nothing which received their approval.

I soon realized that not only was I not in sympathy with their obtuse refusal to fit God's life with Caesar's around them, but also that I never would be. I thought they were mad. On their part, they thought that I had not yet 'come out and out on the Lord's side' and was still too much 'of the world'.

The young evangelists not only kept rigidly to their principles but also seemed to invite persecution even when it was not offered. All government forms, for instance, were regarded as a means of witness. Income tax returns and conscription papers and other pink, grey or blue publications in triplicate with a crown and OHMS at the top were treated with contempt.

When asked to write on the dotted line and state who was their employer, the brethren wrote 'God'. The Academy was legally their employer, though to acknowledge this would mean going into a sinners' nest such as a Labour Exchange to get insurance cards. And although most of the students depended on some form of grant, they filled in their income tax returns saying that the source of their income was 'faith'. Dates of birth were given as the date of our conversion—the second birth. For example, under this system I would have given a birthday to show that I was two years old, while an elder in the faith like Brother Perry on the other caravan across the valley, was not quite ten years. Many of the brethren went through stormy tribunals for conscientous objection to military service. Brothers with a penchant for martyrdom, like Perry, cheerfully faced imprisonment rather than deny their faith.

No wonder that the brothers generated an atmosphere of tension which never relaxed. I could feel it on that first evening in that dank church vestry filled with the smell of cooking rice. It persisted until the brothers departed a few days afterwards, leaving me in charge of the caravan mission. Brother William went off with some misgiving, however. He had made 'some lovely converts' during the mission and no doubt felt reluctant to leave their fledgling souls to my obviously inexperienced cure. Nobody likes to see his careful work wantonly destroyed by the ignorance or clumsiness of others.

Brother William had a more direct cause to be uneasy. This was the result of a surprise visitor. Because I was so young yet well over six feet tall, some of the good people who attended the mission's performances declared that I had outgrown my strength. I kept it as close a secret as possible that I was only sixteen and still had a child's ration card. And I kept the secret because I liked to pass for a man of twenty. My appetite, however, could not be concealed. The voracious, unappeasable hunger of sixteen-year-olds came over me like well-calculated assaults from my adversary the Devil. It was fortunate that I was not preparing immediately for the hardships of Africa like Brother William. Consequently, the rice puddings which were intended to keep us going for at least two or three days went with uncontrollable swiftness at one sitting. Sometimes as I dug away at the quarry of rice with my spoon and carried the white chunks as if by conveyor belt to my mouth, I felt the others' eyes fastened on me. But I could not help it. I had to eat. Preaching to empty stomachs was easier than preaching with one.

During Convention Week a farmer's daughter called Sarah bought some books. We spoke and she invited me to her home when I went up to the mission caravan in Brecknockshire. And so I did go away up into the heart of the Eppynt Hills. I spent such delightful fellowship with her and the family within the snug, strong walls of their farmhouse. Sarah walked me down to the bus afterwards, and lingered as though reluctant to let me go back to our churchyard caravan.

Perhaps her care and interest in me overstepped the permissible limits of sisterly love. One evening, when I returned to the caravan after a service down in Abergavenny, Brother William said he had something to say to me. He had just returned a basket of good things, butter and eggs, fruit and cakes which Sarah had sent down for me from the farm. I could cheerfully have killed Brother William when he said that the woman had brought the basket herself. Although Sarah was at least thirty, Brother William had been shocked that she should burst shamelessly and unchaperoned into an all-male camp. He seemed to be shaken in his former conviction that ours was one of the Lord's stronger strongholds among the back-sliders in the Welsh valleys.

I was not going to disagree with Brother William. In any

case, he was right. Too much worldliness infected my thoughts. Too many carnal desires determined my behaviour. How could I refute his arguments when I had only to glance at the empty rice pudding dish to see the evidence?

Before Brother William would be allowed to let the bright beams of the Gospel fall on dark Africa, he was to attend the School of Tropical Medicine. And before doing this he was determined to shrive me. However, in connection with his medical studies, Brother William had absorbed a certain amount of physiotherapy. His massage had to be practised and to show my humility in the Lord's service, I surrendered myself as a guinea-pig. And while he thumped and kneaded, Brother William subjected my soul to similar treatment. Naturally, my young body responded well to his manipulation. About his effect on my soul I was not so certain. But his massage was so efficient that it stimulated my body and made even sharper the desires against which he preached as he pummelled.

This unfortunate paradox resolved itself when Brother William left our mission station for the last time and made his way down to Abergavenny. No more would our churchyard caravan rock on its springs while he massaged. Presumably he took his skill to the dark continent. During the eighteen years that have passed since, I have often wondered how many young West Africans have been reduced to mental states as confused and self-accusing as mine under Brother William's influence.

Christ flogged the money-changers out of the temple. William, no doubt, chased the Africans' gods and fetishes away. If he did this with as much enthusiasm as he showed over my neckties, the gods probably left in haste. My collection of gaudy ties reminded Brother William of his 'worldly' days in a London broker's office. And although they were perfectly innocuous, both in themselves and by their complete absence of any suggestiveness, sexual or otherwise, the ties had to go, Isaac-wise, to a sacrificial pyre as burnt offerings. Only there was no last-minute reprieve by divine intervention. Between the vestry and the earth closet a little flame leaped up and an oily yellow cloud of smoke spiralled into the still summer air.

Apples of Gold

To be consistent, Brother William should have burnt the earth closet as well as my neckties. And perhaps he would have done, had I poured all my shortcomings into my father confessor's ear. But there again, I drew shrinking back from the brink of total immersion in unworldliness. I simply could not repeat to Brother William the thoughts which seized me when seated in the earth closet. This was not because I was sensitive, but because *he* was. My back street days as a young boy in Belfast had at least taught me that bodily functions were nothing much to worry about either way, worthy of neither undue sensibility nor preoccupation. A long indoctrination in a certain biased version of Christianity countered this learning gleaned from street gangs. So that on occasions, unpredictably and inexplicably, my mind was obsessed by ideas or images in some way connected with those parts of the body known as 'private'. Perhaps the very privacy was itself the main attraction. Who at sometime or another has not peeped through the keyhole of a locked door?

The particular obsession connected with the earth closet was a fairly innocent one, though it was not untouched by Luther-like overtones. Satan's brown bottom seemed to pursue me at every street corner marring my witness, as the monk of Wittenberg believed. However, at the caravan the vision concerned two old ladies. Both were deaconesses and both came to our lonely church on Sunday morning. Their peculiar distinction lay in the fact that they, and they alone, used the two-seater earth closet together.

At that time, my mental make-up consisted in a large degree of curiosity. And I was insatiably curious as to what the old ladies did in there together. And why together? The only thing I could think of was that they went in to read the 'Apples of Gold' in each other's company. Apart from the Apples, the earth closet certainly provided no other reading matter. The Apples of Gold in Pictures of Silver in non-evangelical language, was a common or garden wall calendar bearing scriptural texts for every day of the year. The calendar had long been a favourite in evangelical households. Even for churchyard earth closets in remote Welsh valleys the Apples of Gold infused the common things of life with the Gospel message.

My interest in the old ladies and their Sunday duet on the two-seater was soon superseded by fascination at another presence in the churchyard. At first, there were only signs, a mere hint that I was not, after all, alone when the other brothers left me. As though he were no more than an unhappy wraith exhuded from some dark grave, Abraham hovered about the mission station.

Brother William had irritated rather than inspired me, yet I missed him and felt lonely with only the mountain wind and small creatures in the hedges for company. Brother Stephen went off too and no replacement of him was promised for at least a month. So the churchyard, the vestry-kitchen and the Gospel caravan were mine to command. Mission business filled most of the day. Climbing into a fresh pulpit to face a fresh audience gave me a thrill and sense of power which almost made the evening loneliness worthwhile. But only almost.

When the new converts went off to their homes (many of them, I believe now, were professional converts who got themselves 'saved' at frequent intervals) and when the elders had sung the doxology and gone home to huge suppers of bread and cheese, I was left feeling empty and insufficient. It was then that I had to cycle through the evening lanes to churchyard and to bed.

Cycling was more difficult going home to the caravan than leaving it because there were so many steep hills. While pushing my bike up the winding roads I had plenty of time to look about me, to drink in the summer evening beauty, and to look at the people I passed simply as people and not as prospective clients for my mission. And I envied them. I envied their freedom. Those travellers on the evening lanes were like figures in a painting, they moved in another world from mine. Just as the artist's canvas separates his world from the spectator's, so the people I passed on my way home lived in a blissful unawareness of the strains and stresses I suffered in the service of God, or what I imagined was the service of God.

I even envied the Italian prisoners of war going home to their camp. Their dignified, chocolate-coloured cloaks struck a curiously autumnal note in the blue-grey landscape. Nobody in the district knew much of what tne Italians felt about the fortunes of war. The long cloaks seemed to cover their thoughts also. But sometimes they looked at me and smiled and in the shining black eyes I saw a happiness, a freedom from tension, which I envied and which I seldom now saw on evangelical faces.

In those languorous summer days when a sweetness came down on the mountain airs, sun-tanned youths cycled along the lanes with their tents and camping equipment fixed on the carriers and drinking-bottles on the handlebars. And then I knew how weak in the faith I was. Brother William would have prayed for these sinners. But I envied them their sinners' freedom. I envied the way they threw off respectability and rode about the countryside wearing nothing except their shorts. How I wanted to throw off my hideous black evangelical suit and let my own body grow healthy in the sun. When I trudged up to the waiting caravan I wanted to fling my Bible into the hedge and join the carved mahogany limbs spinning towards the forest night.

Arriving at my eerie site and preparing my lonely supper, I yearned for someone to talk to. But there was nobody. Or was there? The realization that unseen eyes were watching me, following me about the place, came late one evening when I went out of the church. Supper done, I thought I would entertain myself by trying to play a hymn or two on the organ. When the pleasure palled I went out to the earth closet. And there I found something which made my heart stand still. The date on the wall calendar had suddenly jumped forward a couple of months.

Last time I had gone in there, the calendar's uppermost page showed the correct date in July. After Brother Stephen left I tore each day's page from the calendar with meticulous care. I did this to link my isolated camp with the normal world, as castaways on desert islands cut notches in palm trunks. To find, therefore, a whole wodge of Golden Apples torn off and July transposed to September, gave me, as the two-seater deaconesses would have described it, quite a turn.

The pages could only have been removed by human agency, for I automatically dismissed the idea of ghosts. But what sort of person could it be, who would slip into my earth closet, remove a whole two months of calendar texts and steal away leaving no trace behind? I had never known anybody to come into the churchyard, for it lay remotely, approached by a rambling, twisting lane which itself branched off a seldom-frequented minor road. And certainly no local farmworker was so dainty as to even dream of using the two-seater when there were miles of open country where he could do whatever he wanted to in complete isolation.

I was on edge for several days and although not exactly keeping watch, I was alert for further signs of the unidentified visitor. Then, one morning as I walked from the caravan, between the sun-speckled uncut grass, I saw him. He was standing by a corner of the church, wild and magnificent. Black-purple hair sprouted thickly from his head and fell over his brow. A black beard ran riot from ear to ear hiding the thick, strong neck which I suspected was as dirty as the hands which rhythmically rubbed corn just plucked from the field beyond the churchyard hedge. Before I could speak he became aware of me. Two black eyes swept swiftly over my face, dropped to scan my clothes, then, like the eyes of a cornered wild animal, returned to glare fiercely into mine.

He flung the corn away and fled. He leapt over the ditch and made his way along the hedge. He vanished through it. I stood still, not sure whether I was afraid or not. An idea lurked that he might return at dead of night to murder me. Although he had stayed long enough for me to get an impression of him, I could not tell whether he was mad or not. Something about him, a kind of desperate air, made me certain he was no ordinary tramp.

Local farmers had often told me of army deserters who lived in the mountains round about. They were rarely seen. But occasionally the houses were broken into or birds were missing from the chicken runs. According to some reports a few of these deserters had lived native in the hills for years.

I knew what the general attitude to deserters was. I also knew what my own attitude as the Lord's chosen minister should be, for I had heard Brother Perry carry on about them often enough while I visited the other caravan. But though I said nothing, instead of agreeing that these soldiers were to be numbered amongst the blackest of sinners, I secretly felt sorry for them. I failed to see why the mission brothers condemned deserters for hating war when they themselves demanded the right to conscientious objection. Also, I felt sorry because the soldiers would never be able to return to normal life again unless they became prisoners. Rain and storm chased them from hole to hole in the mountainside. Hunger might drive them down to outlying farms to steal food and clothes. Loneliness made them risk capture by hanging about places where a fellow human being might be.

My secret sympathy with the mountain deserters was not defensible by argument. Yet I knew myself what it was to be on the wrong side of the fence from authority. Before the threat of German bombs sent me off to Fermanagh, much of my boyhood had passed with gangs which roamed Belfast's railway verges and met in forbidden or derelict warehouses to plan trouble. Although I knew them well enough, policemen were no friends of mine. Too often I had stolen from market stalls and breadservers' vans during boyhood ever to think of reporting the wild churchyard intruder. What did it matter if I noticed that every day milk was surreptitiously taken from the can standing in the cool church porch?

Several more days passed and although the signs continued, I did not see the man. He left unmistakable traces of himself. Not only was half of my milk taken, but the Apples of Gold began to disappear from the earth closet at an astonishing rate. The milk I could understand, but not the Apples of Gold.

I could even understand the tin of frogs which he left behind on that morning when I surprised him. It seemed unlikely that he had put the frogs in the churchyard as a curse on me. As a child I had hunted in the Bog Meadows of Belfast's waste lands for the biggest and most grotesque frogs I could find. They were to be used in bringing curses down on my hated schoolteachers. But why should my mysterious and mostly-invisible companion of the churchyard wish to curse me? After all, I continued to leave the milk where he could help himself, and after that first morning I left food there also, which was always gone when I returned in the evening. More probably his tin of frogs was fishing bait, as I had used frogs many a time on the end of my crude line when fishing Fermanagh's rivers.

All these things could be interpreted easily. But what about the Apples of Gold? My wild man could not be stealing the scriptural texts to read them. I had to wait a few more days for the explanation. Meanwhile, the feeling of being constantly watched while I was at the caravan and of having my things tampered with when I was not, began to get me down. But I scorned the idea of reporting the man either to the police or to the other mission brothers across the valley. So I decided to wait and face him. Better, I thought, to be murdered in broad daylight by somebody I could see than in the middle of the night by somebody I could not.

Since I had been in the hills, hardly a breath of wind had disturbed the stillness. An ambient calm possessed the air, and azure possessed the sky. Because of this benign stillness, I could tell whenever the wild man had been in the churchyard. After his visits the air was enriched by a kind of incense. I thought at first that he lit fires, perhaps to boil a can of tea. But however hard I searched I could find no tell-tale patches of ash. And then, one evening, when I returned earlier than usual, I smelt the pungent smoke and knew that the secret intruder had either just vanished on hearing me, or was still somewhere in the churchyard.

Before I had wheeled my bicycle to the caravan I saw him standing again in the same place. His eyes shone from the black mass of hair. I spoke to him. He did not reply, but neither did he run off. Instead, he leaned against the wall, smoking. I thought it rather a shocking thing for him to be smoking at all, but to be doing it in a churchyard while leaning against the church itself, seemed the worst of all possible sins.

Some echo sounded in my mind, though, an echo of bygone and happy days. The wild stranger might have been one of my own childhood's tinker friends, grown up now. So although he continued to puff at his straggly, home-made cigarette, I did not chide him as a young student of evangelical theology should have done. In fact, I forgot my position as a missionary and became myself for once. The wild man fascinated me and I wanted to know him, especially as he wore a little gold ring in one ear.

With the fewest possible words I asked him to share some rice pudding and we went together into the vestry to make it. He told me his name. I liked it, and in some unaccountable way it fitted him—Abraham.

Abraham did not talk much. But his was not the taciturnity of the suspicious, but the reticence of the man who lives much alone in lonely places. I did not mind. Tinkers in their rag tents or gypsies in grandiose rococo caravans had been my earliest friends on Belfast's Bog Meadows. The fine faces with high cheekbones and hair as wild as the wild eyes, could not be hidden by rags. All we children knew that gypsies were outcasts and therefore to be feared.

But I too had been an outcast. Trudging the wet Belfast streets, I too went from door to door. But unlike the gypsies I was not trying to tell fortunes but to seek one in the form of a penny. My sisters and I were labelled 'parish orphans' following the death of our window-cleaner father at twenty-seven years. I had a card given me by the Protestant Orphan Society. And I had to go from door to door with this card, collecting pennies for the Society. For each penny, a square on the card was pierced with a pin.

I resented everything to do with the pin-hole card. I hated going up the front paths of the posh semi-detached houses across the River Blackstaff and getting the front door slammed in my face. Also, I hated going to school, for if I needed a new penny jotter, the teacher was angry because she had to fill in a special form so that I could get it for a halfpenny from the parish poor-box. There being few things colder than charity, it was no wonder I was drawn by the warmth of the tinkers' undemanding friendliness. It did not matter to me that they seldom washed and that they lay about on filthy mattresses around the hundred-eyed fire.

When I found that Abraham had no harm in him, and as soon as he knew he could trust me, we became friends. It was as though we had known each other for years. And so I did not pass the evenings alone any more in the Gospel caravan, flicking over the pages of my Bible concordance and making sermon notes. Instead I kept the oil-lamp burning far longer than the Academy would have thought proper.

While Abraham's black eyes flashed at me across the tiny table, I talked in torrents about my 'unsaved' days. The Fermanagh summer dusks had been so beautiful to me when the war pitched me out of the city into the West's countryside. I loved the gathering nights not only because of the illegal season of the yellow eels, but because it was a man's right to be abroad at night with his traps and snares. Nor had these activities been mere hobbies. The money I earned from the sale of rabbits and fox skins had gone towards buying my black and unbecoming evangelical clothes.

Abraham seemed not to care that I was supposed to be a dedicated young man. He showed not the slightest awe at the evidence of holiness around him in the form of Bibles and hymn-books and edifying propaganda. But he listened intently as I talked about the building of wattle weirs for fishing or of burning rivers with oil-soaked turves at night to spear salmon.

In his turn, Abraham talked of the Welsh mountains and of breaking horses, Appleby Fair, the New Forest, and of charcoal-burning days in boyhood. I never knew a more knowledgeable herbalist, in spite of being brought up to have more faith in plants than doctors. Of the future, Abraham would say nothing. A shadow remained drawn over this, as shadows often stood on one mountain flank while across the valley

another was bathed in sunlight. Did he dream of a place in the
world and among his own tribe when the war ended? At the
moment he knew his tribe would not hesitate to hand him over
to the authorities, for he had first of all abandoned it for tragic
reasons. Would Abraham ever return to the peafields and find
a bride from his own people, one with a dowry of skewbald
ponies, bantam cocks and a string of lurcher dogs?

I was glad of Abraham's company, and at first I regarded it as
a way to relieve the monotony of lonely evenings. But in the
end I began to enjoy being with him and roaming about over
the hills more than going off by bicycle to the various parts of
my mission field. We began to spend much of the day together
also. Souls meekly striving in the Welsh valleys, so carefully
nurtured by my zealous predecessors, began to be neglected.

Although the weeks rushed by and I began to think vaguely
about the beginning of the Bible Academy's autumn term, I
was perfectly happy with Abraham. And it would have been an
insult to try and convert him. In any case, I should not have
liked him so much if he *had* been converted. This disturbing
idea occasionally threatened the contentment of that high
summer. But I easily thrust it aside, refusing to see myself as a
salesman who did not believe in the value of the goods he sold.

A much more disturbing idea, however, had to be grappled
with. This was the possibility of an imminent return by Brother
William to see how his 'lovely little converts' were progressing
along the path of faith. I was terrified of him appearing suddenly one evening and finding a sinner of such dimensions
as Abraham sitting on his caravan bunk. This problem was
solved by Abraham sleeping in the church, wrapped in a sleeping-bag on a pew and looking exactly like a chrysalis in a pupa
case.

Worse, worse by far, if Brother William had decided on a
Second Coming, would have been the smoking. The smell of
Abraham's home-made herbal tobacco pervaded the whole
churchyard. Evangelical noses were as well trained to detect
the presence of tobacco as the Inquisition's nose was to detect
the presence of heresy. And not the least alarming aspect of

Abraham's smoking was the way he dropped crumbs of tobacco everywhere when he rolled his cigarettes. I even found occasional shreds lurking between the pages of my Bible when I opened it to address a meeting down the valley.

Black and heinous though the sin of smoking was, much blacker and more heinous was the sin of what he rolled his cigarettes in. For, within a few minutes of actually making friends with Abraham, the mystery of the missing Apples of Gold was solved. The calendar pages were of the exact dimension and thickness required of a cigarette paper. Without the slightest sense of sacrilege Abraham rolled his herbal tobacco in the Apples of Gold and puffed away to his heart's content. Naturally I could not allow him to smoke inside the Gospel caravan, for his mountain-grown herbs had a peculiarly persistent smell. And I also did my best to dissuade him from smoking in the church when he settled into his sleeping-bag for the night.

And what would Sister Winifred and her husband have said had they seen the Gospel caravan's rice pots and dishes being used for such exotic fare? No one would have believed the richly garnished omelettes had come from moorhens' eggs with creamed fern fronds or fried lichen. Certainly nothing at the Bible Academy had tasted so good as the richly stuffed hedgehog earth-baked and served with thick snail gravy.

Abraham was a secret. I mentioned him to nobody. Once, before I got to know him and became his friend, I had hinted at his presence to Sister Edna. This lady was living on a farm on the mountain side of the valley. The caravan missioners went up and used her place as a rallying point, for Sister Edna could report to the Academy, obtain funds for us and give us hot baths.

Once upon a day, Sister Edna was a fellow deaconess of Sister Winifred. But where the Principal's wife was sour and crabbed and bitter and filled with a desire to see the wicked suffering in hell, Sister Edna was radiant with genuine love. She was so busy trying to flood the world with love that she had no time left for obsession about sin. Although I could not foresee the vicissitudes of my future or the strange, winding patterns the river of my life was to make through the landscape of passing years, Sister Edna remained my constant friend, and still is as a very old lady today.

She and her husband had started an orphanage and holiday homes for poor children in Devon. Those homes called Child Haven on the sands of County Down, where I had spent childhood summers, were similar and I knew how much Sister Edna's good works meant to the children. But now she lived on the farm up the valley because her own grand house had been turned into yet another home for Dr. Barnardo.

When Sister Edna cycled perilously down to the caravan loaded with pies and baskets of fruit for me, she did not notice the poached pheasant's feathers still lying about or the dirty dishes. She came only to give her friendship in the same way as Abraham.

But nobody could have denied that happy though I was, apostasy had settled like thick dust over the mission station. The time was indeed ripe for the coming of a new brother, strong and without tarnish on his heavenly armour. My days, in other words, with Abraham were numbered, and came to an abrupt end when Brother Edward came up from Abergavenny.

Brother Edward was prevented by an aura of heroism which did not all displease me. During the Convention Week I had heard a lot about Brother Edward. Like myself he would be a freshman when the Academy began its new session. Unlike most of the other students, however, Brother Edward did not come from an accountant's office or a public school but from the sea. He was a real sailor. His conversion had been a quite spectacular one and even took place, or as near as made no difference, on a Biblical site, namely in the Red Sea. I knew all this from one of the more popular pamphlets circulated during Convention Week, which dealt with Brother Edward's forsaking of the world. Climbing one day into the crow's nest as his ship ploughed its way down the Red Sea, he found a New Testament deposited there by a port evangelist. He saw the light in a flash and Edward the Sailor became Edward the

Saved, and found his way to the Bible Academy when the navy discharged him as medically unfit.

And anybody could see the sea in Edward's blue eyes and fresh sailor's face. The Christian clothes he wore too had almost a salty tang about them, or more strictly speaking an American swing, for Edward's mouth, besides being full of praises, was also full of names quite new to me, names such as Billy Graham and the Moody Bible Institute. Clearly my own experience of evangelism was as out-dated and dowdy as the brown-dadoed mission halls I spoke in. Edward, apparently, had done wonderful work among American servicemen in Bournemouth. And the moment the war ended he would be off to Chicago to the famed Moody Institute. Before Brother Edward's first week elapsed I had also decided to apply to the Moody Institute. Though, of course, I had not as yet been to America, it definitely seemed now that Chicago had something which Wales had not.

Meanwhile, the labourers had their Welsh vineyard to think about. We roared and pleaded in a score of more-than-sleepy villages and, true sailor that he was, Edward took me farther and farther afield. The pulpits grew bigger and bigger, the churches and chapels loftier and filled with even-more-important congregations. Even the nature of postal deliveries to the mission station changed. Almost every day now exotic literature poured in for Edward from America. I began to have visions of other sheep which were not of my fold. I saw the thousands of Americans who were all on the Lord's side.

Everything Edward did was done with a dash and flair which could not but appeal even to the most hardened of sinners. And this being so, what could I do but fall over backwards in admiration? The backsliding into which I had fallen had to be rectified immediately. So without ado I stopped going with Abraham first thing in the morning down to the river where we had been in the habit of taking a shamelessly naked bath. Instead I accompanied Brother Edward when he went to take a good, Christian, hot bath at Sister Edna's farm.

But Brother Edward had a more serious effect on my career

as an evangelist. My reasons for wanting to be posted to Africa as a missionary were not completely altruistic. I had always wanted to travel. When I left Ireland god-speeded by various evangelical well-wishers and sponsors, it was a foregone conclusion that I would end up among the 'black folk' in Africa. Now, however, Brother Edward opened up new horizons, wide American horizons. The awe and respect I previously held for the great names of the Keswick Convention began to fade. American's hottest soul-savers became my heroes. I too began to feel irked that the war dragged on so, preventing me from getting into Chicago's Moody Bible Institute.

By God's providence, it seemed, at the moment there was no need to go across the Atlantic to save American souls. Dozens of Yankee boats docked at Swansea and Cardiff. American servicemen crowded the pavements, and all awaited our personal ministry.

Brother Edward never forgot the means of his conversion in the Red Sea, nor had I forgotten my first months at work on board a mud-dredger in Belfast Lough. The sea was our common bond. New zeal bubbled in me. And as a sign I locked the two-seater earth closet every night to save the Apples of Gold from further desecration.

CHAPTER III

Shamrock

❧❦❧

Summer done, the Bible Academy awaited us, along with winter and frozen morning prayers. The building which housed the Academy adequately expressed what went on behind those graceless façades. Originally, in the 1920s, it had been destined as an hotel. And although this was linked in our minds with sin the connection was tenuous. Luxury would hardly have been the keynote of that hotel. Even our roll of alumni which shone with glories won by ex-students in every corner of the evangelical world, could not alleviate the drab atmosphere.

I have never quite been able to free myself from some notion, derived in my childhood, that a house demonstrates its degree of luxury by its bathroom. At our Academy, the one bathroom was shared between all staff and students, except for the Vice-Principal who was an up-to-date cleric from Cambridge with a bathroom to himself, and it gave the exact tone of the place.

Hence, the bath rota. It hung among the crowded time-table notice-board which gave the times and places of classes in pastoral theology and homiletics, Greek and Hebrew, textual criticism and canon law, French and Spanish. The rota told us at which quarter-of-an-hour we could take our four-and-a-half inches of warm water for our weekly bath. The Rev. Principal himself had painted the blue Plimsoll line in the bath. Not for us was the lying back, the soaking of a relaxed body in steaming water, as though we were just so many godless film stars.

This bathroom parsimony proved my theory. The Academy's whole way of life followed the bathroom pattern. And here I could see the seeds of conflict being sown. Brother Edward had not been a sailor for nothing. Ships and the sea had taught him to look after Number One. And no true evangelical could blame him for that, because self-preservation ('personal salvation' sounded less selfish, but amounted to the same thing) was a fundamental of evangelical doctrine. Edward, however, with his modern and American outlook, could not see why the Academy should expect its students to live like the inmates of a Victorian workhouse. Disregarding the virtues of poverty and humility he sneaked into the kitchen and stoked up the boiler before having his bath. Edward was also found out on a number of occasions using outrageous quantities of hot water for washing-up while on pantry duty.

Paradoxically, pleasure was taken out of the fact that the Academy had been designed as an hotel. The Principal derived the greatest satisfaction, for he saw the Lord's hand at work. He thought of God as being like a good goblin who arranged things nicely in a fairy story. In His mercy and wisdom He had foiled the plans of the hotel proprietors. Instead of being a sinner's nest the place had become a home for Christians on a full-time training course. To prove that the Lord had other ideas, the Principal would pat the top of an oddly-shaped shelf in his office. Do you know what this is, he would ask freshmen. Well, it was a bar counter. And the Lord had set His seal on the building, he said, because not a single pint of beer had ever been served across that bar. The licensing of the hotel had been resolutely and successfully opposed by local Christians. The building would have become a white elephant but for the Academy. 'They thought they were building a public house, but God knew they were building a Bible School', the Principal said years later in *The Life of Faith*, the evangelical journal.

Evangelicals were apt to go apoplectic at the mention of alcohol. Only one thing was worse than alcohol and that was sexual intercourse. But sex was so bad that the only way to deal with this was to pretend it did not exist at all. Alcohol, however,

39

was always with us. I was reminded of this on the first Friday of every month—our Day of Prayer. The Principal trudged along the dank passages and himself cut up tiny cubes of bread for holy communion. Then, again personally, he carried a tray laden with little glasses for the non-alcoholic wine which formed the sacrament's second part. Our communion was taken in the big lecture hall. Chapel and communion rail were alike spurned. Christ Himself had instituted the occasion in an upper room and we recalled this by celebrating amongst the desks and music stands.

As the Principal put the little glass of insipid wine before each student he might have passed as any retired longshoreman of the neighbourhood or a gardener up in the allotments. The Principal was perfectly aware of his appearance. Worldliness had to be avoided at all cost, even to the extent that although he was ordained, like all the other lecturers, he did not wear clerical clothes. If he looked like a gardener so much the better, for was not Christ mistaken for a gardener on the first Easter Sunday morning? This polemical attitude to dress was reinforced by further arguments. Who, the Principal would demand, could make such a mistake about the Bishop of Rome or the Incumbent of Canterbury?

How glad I was when our Day of Prayer was done, when the students with violins opened their cases for the amber discs of rosin, when the piano lid was opened and when the Principal arranged himself at the organ. Any instrument available was employed not merely to fill the great hall (ex-hotel ballroom) but to send the message out through the windows, across the street, and into the windows of the Conservative Club where the miners and dockers were drinking themselves into perdition. At the sound of our praise the drinkers could not but know that the Lord Omnipotent reigneth.

Sometimes at this hour we would sing hymns with popular tunes. Normally, and unfortunately, we used our own college hymn-book which contained translations by the Principal from Welsh or French into the pidgin-English perfected in the last century for use in hymns. We were expected to read music so that we could tackle the more obscure tunes. Besides the hymn-book we each carried a file containing hand transcriptions by the Principal on variegated, multi-coloured scraps of paper, of tunes which may well, and probably did, come out of the Ark.

Although the Academy smelt of carbolic soap and parochialism we had international affiliations, notably with Switzerland. An establishment at Geneva similar to ours was our main contact. Our days began with readings from the Geneva Daily Bible Portions in the dining-hall. By half-past eight our own private meditations were complete, as well as a cold hour in the lecture hall before domestic chores and breakfast. The long day which began in the lecture hall sometimes went on until nine in the evening. With a speed which impeded scholarship we imbibed the history of missions, we became steeped in the fallacies of modern heresies, we mugged-up doctrine and church history. What a relief it was when we closed our note-books and went into the town to practise our learning on the cinema queues, or to spend an hour or so in the carpenter's shop.

On Wednesdays the hierarchy allowed us a few free hours when we could go shopping or stay in and do our personal laundry. Wednesdays became a busy day for me. I went to Sisterhoods and Mothers' Unions and soon installed myself as a favourite speaker. These collections of lonely, middle-aged women with little to fill their lives, loved to hear about the pomegranates I had left behind in Ireland, the juicier the better.

But come seven on a Wednesday evening everyone was in his place again with ears pinned back for the Principal's weekly Biblical Exegesis. Being something of a highspot, the Wednesday evening affair was attended by slight deviation from routine. The gas stove was turned up higher than its customary glimmer because outsiders came in to hear the celebrated Bible teacher.

It was at Wednesday's session that once more I allowed Satan to possess me. I had eyes for nothing but the outsiders, or rather, for one of them. All around me the India-paper Bible pages were flicked over, making a susurrant sound like a calm

41

sea. The Principal's voice droned on and on. Sunday school teachers and church elders worked pencils rhythmically across notebooks. But I was staring at Monica. She was the most beautiful creature ever to be seen inside our dreary building.

Monica not only bowled me over, she gave me a challenge. And I was faced with a problem of monumental proportions. Should I attempt to walk Monica home? She was engaged to Brother Stephen who was away in Scotland and therefore unable himself to escort her. Moreover, Wednesday was the week's sole evening when we could miss our supper of cocoa with bread and mix. As things turned out, Monica found me a school-friend to walk home. But on the second occasion, there was a better conclusion. Poor Monica saw me bidding her friend good night and was so overcome with jealousy that she told her friend that I had made overtures to her, Monica, first. My stratagem worked perfectly. The politics of love are simple. Within a few Wednesdays, my socks were being carried home in Monica's Bible wallet to be washed and darned.

The three Fridays of the month which were not Days of Prayer were generally voted as the most interesting. Of course, they ended with a prayer meeting as usual, but at least we had a tangible target for our prayers. This was nothing less important than the week-end engagement list.

Theological students were welcomed into churches and chapels not only because fully-fledged ministers were unobtainable, but because, often as not, the churches and chapels could not afford them. Decrepitude had crept up on the majority of these places. Many of them could afford no more than the student's train fare. Those which could give their preachers a modest fee were quickly snatched up. It was interesting to see the regularity with which the Spirit led some of our best preachers to accept engagements at the churches which paid most.

After the first weeks of the term I was never anxious to stray far from the Academy. A pulpit at the Navvy Mission or Sailors' Rest was good enough for my Sunday. My experiences farther afield with all-day Sunday engagements, soon lacked lustre. I always seemed to end up in the same sort of conventicle, followed by the same sort of farmhouse dinner, and afterwards the same sort of walk to chapel again with the elders, to stand and speak on the same kind of platform where the same sort of water carafe, lined with bubbles, stood on faded green baize.

Had there not been such a strong counter-attraction I might have continued with my Sunday forays into the countryside, up the hills and down the valleys. But the docks lay within siren distance of the Academy. And these were irresistible.

On the term's first Saturday, the Principal had taken Brother Edward and me to be interviewed for our passes into the docks, because war-time security was still strict. Once in my pocket, the pass burned me much more than did my Bible. Blustering winds whipped smartly off the sea and whistled through a tangle of masts and aerials bringing autumn and the threat of winter gales. I was filled with ecstasy as I made my way towards the anchored ships.

The American liberty boats were to be my pulpit. Brazilian donkeymen were my elders. Beer-swigging Danes pronounced a new kind of benediction. The Arab boys, the sailors' peggies, the Indian 'chippies', the dope peddlars, the Cockney 'sparks', the money-changing Canadians, the sweating Scots wipers, were to be my flock or so I thought.

Perhaps I had never felt so much pride as that first time when I climbed a rope ladder, bearing the bright pink pass of a port missionary. I was genuinely full of determination to do a bit of 'groping for Jesus'. Not knowing precisely what to expect, I had donned the armour of readiness. But I had reckoned without the fabulous American genius for friendliness. Also, I had not calculated how different an American liberty ship would be from a Belfast dredger.

Edward and I were not exactly piped aboard. But neither were we laughed to scorn, nor, what was worse in evangelical eyes, ignored. No sooner were our feet measuring that immaculate deck than our literature was hungrily seized, while we ourselves were swept off to demolish an outsize American navy repast punctuated by cups of strong coffee. Meanwhile, word went round the ship that strangers were on board, an occurrence rare enough in war-time to make us a centre of interest in the messroom.

But none of the Americans could have been as impressed with me as I was by them. In fact the brightness and air of efficiency, the warmth and friendliness, the relaxed youthful atmosphere, impressed me more than anything had since the day when I was a back-street evacuee of twelve suddenly confronted with the gracious luxury of a country rectory. The contrast, of course, between the monastic sparseness of the Academy with the liberal generosity of the American naval way of life, was too much for me. I forgot about trying to glow as a winner of souls. The tattoos on the torsos of young sailors coming from hot shower-baths, fascinated me much more than the Gospel seals for sticking on letters home, which Edward was trying to sell.

I began to understand Edward's enthusiasm for things American. From the messroom I went from cabin to cabin, ostensibly to sell Bibles and *The Sailor's Guide*. But I found that my address book began to fill up. I could not resist writing down such poetry as Arizona, Dakota, Minnesota, Nebraska, Missouri. Almost greedily I wrote down the sailors' home addresses, so that I could send the Gospel good news to their unconverted womenfolk back in the States.

Flushed with triumph at this first visit, I returned to the Academy. Our dockland efforts were received with hallelujahs. The Word was going out to the high seas and the dollars were coming in.

Concerning my own inner feelings, I remained silent. What could I say? It was clearly impossible to confess that I had in fact begun to backslide again. Before leaving the liberty ships the sailors had given me money so that I could go and buy presents for their girl-friends—the sort of presents which certainly could never be bought in a Bible shop.

The following Sunday morning revealed the fruits of our labours. A dozen American sailors trooped into the Academy hall looking for Eddie and Bob. They brought with them the fresh draughtiness of the sea and the comradeship of those that go down to the sea in ships. They created quite a stir in our dingy midst. Even Sister Winifred's firm Christian jaw did not sag when she was asked if she would like to chew gum. I wore what I hoped was an impassive mask betokening my possession of the peace which passeth understanding. Actually, I was suffering torments of nervous tension. I was terrified lest some careless sailor should forget my injunctions about smoking while in our building. At any moment I was expecting to see a hand go to a breast pocket and draw out the Luckies. It *was* a lucky strike that none of them did.

How proud Brother Edward and I were, sitting in our church among our sheep in their spotless, tight-fitting uniforms. Looked at on the lowest level we had saved the sailors from at least a couple of hours among Bute Street's whore houses. And like financiers reviewing their investments, we wondered how many of today's contacts would lead to the glory of a soul saved for all eternity. Looking at the bewildered but intent sea-tanned faces it was not easy to forget Edward's conversion up in the crow's nest nor my own salvation effected not so long before in a Belfast city mission, whither the hand of a pimply shop-girl whom I then fancied had led me.

Neither Edward nor I were preaching during that week-end so we took the sailors off to the town's high spot of evangelism. But before we lit our gas brackets at the Bible Academy that night the first storm had broken over my head. When the Americans had gone back to their ships and Edward settled down to deal with his vast pile of correspondence, I felt unaccountably desolate.

During tea, the other students talked about their morning engagements and of where they would spend the evening Gospel Hour. Since the Academy was nominally inter-denominational, I had stated my intention of worshipping as an Anglican, since I had been brought up in the Church of Ireland. But the evangelical churches I had known in Belfast, had no counterpart in the Welsh churches near the Academy. And the

Principal did not approve of my plan, for the parish churches indulged in practices which were unacceptable.

He tried to deflect my interest on to the Navvy Mission, which was conducted approximately along Prayer Book lines. The Mission's founder, besides being a bad poet and a worse painter, was also the man who had bought up the ex-hotel and handed it over to the Academy. On account of this he was held in some esteem by the Principal and staff of the Academy. Whether the founder enjoyed such a reputation elsewhere was open to doubt. For one thing, the Bishop of Llandaff had refused to confirm children prepared at the Navvy Mission, thereby affronting the poet and painter. However, undaunted, the Mission pursued its policy of sticking, more or less, to the Book of Common Prayer. I had no objection to preaching at the Mission on Sunday mornings. But I had no intention of becoming a full member of the congregation. And so I repeated my determination to the Principal.

Over tea on that Sunday, Brother Edward told me that he would be coming with me to the church which I had insisted on attending. Edward was an Anglican himself which was one reason. But also, he said, the Principal had asked him to keep an eye on me.

I blew up.

Some months before leaving Ireland I had applied to the Sacred Mission at Kelham for training as a missionary priest. But the D-Day ban on travelling was on, and I could not cross to England for the necessary personal interview to which Kelham invited me. Nor had I the patience to wait for the ban to end and so snatched at the opportunity of going to the Bible Academy which required no previous interview. And now this self-same Academy had taken on itself to watch me like the Gestapo because I intended worshipping in a church which liked a pinch of popish salt in its Prayer Book porridge. Edward was supposed to keep an eye on *me*—I who had all but got into the Sacred Mission itself, which, even on clear days, could hardly be seen across the River Trent because of the incense clouds around it!

Keep an eye on me indeed! I stormed out of the dining-hall and burst into the Principal's study. I told him a thing or two. Then I rushed out of the Academy and hurried along to the parish church where Benediction was taking place.

I had no difficulty in finding the church because as part of an evangelical guerrilla exercise during the preceding week I had been there with other students to strew Gospel tracts on the pews. And as I sat now on those self-same, desecrated pews, watching the slow movements of the ceremony as the incense dissolved into the dark caverns of the roof, regrets began to creep in. Not theological regrets, but the more urgent and practical ones that perhaps I had ruined my career. I was afraid that my strong words in the Principal's study had brought my student days to an abrupt and untimely end.

Sister Winifred and her husband, however, were terrified of my soul being spirited away by the high-jinks of Canterbury. Many of my fellow students went into deep and long prayer sessions for my deliverance. However, expediency demanded at least the appearance of peace, and so by Monday I was running back to the parish church with a fresh bunch of tracts.

And on this Monday also I missed most of my lectures, because so many American sailors came to buy things from the Bible shop that Sister Winifred could not cope and had to send for me. Before we reached half term I was spending at least three days a week in the docks. And by that time I realized the true nature of my wanderings among the ships. Sure enough, I carried Greek and Dutch Testaments according to the nationality of the boats I would visit. But really I was escaping from the evangelical concentration camp.

Food had a lot to do with it. I was often so hungry that I stole out of the Academy and went to a little dock café used by coloured people and soldiers. It was some consolation to find Brother Edward in there also. But my mind could not keep from picturing the gargantuan meals on board the ships where butter was unrationed and a cup of real coffee could be turned into syrup with as much sugar as was needed to make the spoon stand up.

The Academy people were always talking about life abundant. But I found more abundant life in the ships then ever I did in our mean building and meaner lives. It was natural that I should be drawn to the raucous, roaring, full-blooded life of the docks. I was sixteen and eager for whatever life could offer from its grotequely overfull coffers. And the degree of my apostasy could be gauged from the fact that I began not to care whether my friends on board were 'saved' or not.

Like a good salesman, I still cleared my case of Bibles and books from the depot by the end of each day. But when the sailors offered me gifts of rationed food, I did not refuse as I should have done. Instead I walked brazenly out through the dock gates bearing such forbidden luxuries as a white loaf or a pound of butter. Even Sister Winifred, a Christian half-a-century strong, became interested and expectant over the possible contents of the Bible case on my return.

One-way traffic through the docks gates could easily become two-way. Very soon, among the Russian Bibles and Portuguese Gospels a few combs and nail brushes were concealed for use on the bodies whose souls were supposed to be my primary concern. And nail brushes were only the start.

Although I may not have dared to stare the fact in the face, I became aware that the twelve foundations of the Heavenly City were not as solid as I had been led to believe. There were serious cracks in them. With my background of poverty I knew that whatever else might change with changing beliefs, money would not. I began to desire money, not for itself, but for its invulnerability.

This discovery coincided with my discovery of a new world in Cardiff.

My port sales were so successful that I persuaded the Principal to get me a pass into the Cardiff Docks. They had the advantage of being far enough away from the Academy to allow me freedom. The result was that I found my way to Bute Street. And there it seemed I need travel no farther afield to carry out my missionary career. Bute Street brought the mission field of Africa to my doorstep.

Shamrock

To me, Bute Street was not merely a swarming dockland of seamen's pools, coal-hoists and cranes, of the Shipping Exchange, and of drunken sailors and professional layabouts, of dolly-dives and red biddy parlours. To me, the motley was a continent, all of Africa, all of Asia rolled into one. Bute Town even had its own mosque to call its devout Muslims towards Mecca five times a day, just as we at the Bible Academy fled to the Throne of Grace.

Human flotsam from every sea-going nation in the world jostled in Bute Town's streets and in its bars. Any of a score of languages could be heard in the crowd that surged along the pavements, going in and out of Italian brothels and Chinese laundries, Arab restaurants and Spanish wine shops. Latvians and Irish tinkers rubbed shoulders with the Welsh dockers whose names the port labour officer called for work from his pulpit.

Ballymacarrett docks in Belfast, where I was born, could not hold a candle to old Tiger Bay, which I took to like a fish to water. After all, I had lived in and around docks all my life. Manhood began for me at fourteen years when I walked through the dock gates at Queen's Island to start work. Although being wrenched from Fermanagh was a terrible experience, my first morning in the docks was not without an element of pride. Queen's Island was a man's island. And even while I was an evacuee in the county of lakes I had felt slighted if any of the people in for a *ceili* confessed to not knowing that ships like the *Titanic* had been laid in Belfast, where we built vessels to 'wear out the ocean'.

The lodgers in our little house had always been journeyman painters, caulkers, stevedores. The male members of my father's family had all carried off their midday 'piece' to Queen's Island and had made their black billy-cans sing on the dockside. So Cardiff's Bute Town was home to me in a way that the Bible Academy could never be. And before many months were out, I recognized the changes in myself. The combs hidden under the Bibles in my case became reefers.

But the spiritual cares of my life had not departed. By the

agency of the captain of an American liberty ship, spiritual matters came very much to the fore. He offered me a shot of whisky while he looked through my case of books. Feeling insulted, I refused and offered him a tract about the lake of fire and brimstone prepared for all wine-bibbers. But I had met my match in the captain. Did I know my Bible, he enquired. Then he asked me to point to any passage which denounced strong drink. And attacking instead of defending, he quoted Old Testament references about wine used in offerings and capped his evidence with the marriage at Cana. To confound me further he took a scroll of Hebrew scripture from his locker and laid it with reverence on the table. Before I left his ship I was fairly drunk and carried out the remains of the bottle in my case.

Quite contrary to my intention, the captain had converted *me*. And as in the case of most conversions a remarkable sense of freedom possessed me. Like Bunyon's Pilgrim a burden rolled off my back, the burden of narrow cant and prejudice. I was glad to know that the Bible Academy's God of fear and violence was not, after all, almighty. I was glad that the dusky children along Bute Street would not be going to hell because they had been taught from the Koran. I rejoiced at the emptiness of the Throne of Grace because now my mother would not burn eternally as a result of the few odd bottles of stout on a night out with a boy-friend.

So far as I was concerned, the Academy's God had frizzled himself out in his own fire. Never again would I warn sinners in the Welsh valleys or sailors reeling along the waterfront to flee from wraths to come, for the whole thing was a myth. At last I was free of those childhood nightmares of Christ coming again and finding my mother in the jug and bottle entrance.

In any case, I had studied some Greek before going to the Bible Academy, and knew that the everlasting, 'eternal' fire was a reference to the fire of the Aeons, the consuming divine fire that singed the selfish soul. The illustrative and symbolic ideas of fire in the Old Testament had always fascinated me. And even gentle Jesus, meek and mild, was quoted in the

Gospels as saying to the accursed, depart from me into *the* eternal fire. And when we were children, Belfast's Gospel halls scared us into attendance with such phrases as *eternal damnation, vengeance of eternal fire, punished with everlasting destruction, the lake of fire, to be cast into hellfire,* in fact a regular thesaurus of arson.

When I was a boy riding on the back of the breadserver's horse van, I used to hope that the driver in front on the dickey would get me with his whip which was made especially long to deal with back-riders like me. I preferred to be punished there and then for stealing potato-farls or coconut snowballs than having the punishment deferred until Judgment Day. But the American captain of a liberty ship had changed all that and now I was released from the chains of fear. It seemed inevitable now that the God of Wrath should topple over the edge of his own bottomless abyss.

We were fixed impossibly in a cleft stick in Belfast in those poverty-stricken days of the 1930s. We could not win. I was in such circumstances that often when I was hungry the only thing to do was to steal food, or if we needed coal in the house the only thing to do was to knock a bucketful off one of the goods trains which were always grinding slowly past our house. Not only were we sometimes forced to steal in order to survive but we put our souls in jeopardy by doing so.

Well, the captain had blown hell sky-high for me. Quite suddenly, with the shock of a cold shower-bath, I saw a new Christ, the one who was concerned that the hungry should be fed and the naked clothed and the prisoners visited, and that His wrath concerned those who denied the hungry and the naked. Smoking and drinking just did not come into it. Nor did other subsidiary considerations such as whether you were Protestant or Catholic. I had sometimes felt rather sorry for the Roman Catholics who refused my appeals to get themselves 'saved', and who therefore were destined for the fire.

With the fear of hellfire gone, my ideas about 'second birth' had to be revised. The New Testament faith, *pistis*, was not a hand-raising act in a Gospel hall or tent mission. It was the quality and tone of heart and mind which unlike the sheep, the goats did not possess. What else could I feel now but that I was lacking *pistis* if I gave those morbid Gospel tracts about hell-fire to seamen who were leaving the short-lived safety and pleasure of the Welsh ports for the mine-infested Atlantic? The blue-scarred faces of the miners across the road at the Conservative Club seemed suddenly to have much more in common with the sheep than did the black-hatted elders and soap-smelling deaconesses.

I thought about Abraham up in the hills. By going out fishing all night in the rivers, even though he was poaching, he had more in common with Christ's disciples than had the Academy's prigs of students who regarded my late-night activity with suspicion. Sharp at ten of an evening the Academy's front door was shut, and only when the Lord threatened to break through in revival were the gas brackets allowed to be lit during the unholy hours of night.

I saw later on that I ought to have told them I was through with their self-centred, hypocritical cant and then walked out slamming the door behind me. But where would I have gone? And to do what? So I stayed and began to lead a double life.

I did not lose my love of the pulpit with my belief in hellfire. But under the new conditions the pulpit was no more than a stage and I the sole actor. I got a thrill out of holding an audience at my mercy, though my sermons were markedly milder in the promises about the other life. My vanity knew no bounds, for when cornered one night after a service at Aberthaw by some airmen from St. Athan's camp about being so young looking, I went off the next day and got some spectacles with almost plain lenses which I thought added another five years to my age. This subterfuge remained a favourite trick of mine for years.

I enjoyed my preaching engagements at Aberthaw, despite being bored by Deacon Davis-Davis. Everybody at the Academy knew Deacon Davis-Davis. Physically he was an enormous man and his presence on a Saturday evening when he came in to pick up his Sunday preacher made even my fellow students seem human by comparison. They actually sniggered with a grain of humour discovered somewhere in their seedy souls. But not to laugh at Deacon Davis-Davis would have required superhuman qualities, for the poor man's cross took the form of an outsize and embarrassing rupture.

Unfortunately, the rupture chose to show itself in the chapel more than at any other time or place. Like similar places round about, the chapel was in its declining years, and Sunday school was therefore combined with the morning service. By an old tradition the children read a verse of scripture aloud. But usually, very few stood up to do so at the morning service— except the old deacon. And once begun, nothing it seemed could stop him. He went through whole chapters, quite oblivious of the agony he was causing even the most devout. The Air Force boys I was sure, only came to witness the trials of strength between Deacon Davis-Davis and the preacher of the day. Goya's drawing 'Blind man in love with his hernia', when I saw it years later, reminded me of Deacon Davis-Davis reading at morning service.

Although I tried more than ever now not to go far from the docks and ships, there were week-ends when preaching engagements at some distance from the Academy were unavoidable. But even then I tried to arrange things so that at the least some of my American sailor friends could go with me. Many of these were Baptists themselves but liked a bit of the other sort of fellowship. More usually, however, my navy friends preferred the fellowship of dusky bodies down Bute Street, and liked their communion better in smoky dock pubs. At about this time I became familiar with the Norwegian Seamen's Church whose chapel had a totally different atmosphere from the Sailors' Rests and Seamen's Missions I was accustomed to. And in the white-painted church and among the men in their thick sweaters was germinated my love of Scandinavia which led me later in life to live in Denmark.

Double lives rarely go on for ever. Mine came to an end abruptly at the end of the first term. Although a number of students had invited me to stay at their homes during the vacation, I felt a desperate need to get right away from the

vinegar and gall of the evangelical atmosphere. I was home-
sick. I wanted Ireland. This appeared to be impossible, for
although D-Day was over the travel ban was still partly in
force. In reply to my request for a permit the Liverpool Passport Office informed me that it could only be granted in an
emergency.

I determined to be an emergency.

The problem was, how? Academy examinations were on.
While the other students were sucking their pens over Calvinis-
tics I went out of the building into the square in front. The
morning was cold, wet and wintry. I got ready to swoon. My
fainting fit had to be in full view of the Conservative Club, so
that the outside world would have my interests at heart as well
as the Academy. Remembering to pocket my stage glasses, I
fell to the ground, taking good care not to injure myself in the
process.

The examination hall went into an uproar. The Conservative
Club threw its doors open. Somehow I was snatched into the
Academy before the wine-bibbers could claim me. They put
me on the kitchen table and sent for a doctor. I went through
anxious moments, wondering what Sister Winifred would say
for she regarded the kitchen table as a sort of altar on which
every bone was scraped with Christian care, every slice of roly-
poly carefully gauged as to thickness.

The doctor came and pronounced me the victim of a nervous
breakdown. So I retired with my breakdown, a not uncommon
ailment among students at examination time, to the Principal's
private apartments, where Sister Winifred ministered to my
needs as I lay in bed. When I could do so without raising suspicion I suggested to the doctor that a convalescence in Ireland would put me on my feet again. He agreed and signed the
necessary certificate. The Passport Office capitulated and looking as healthy as I had done at any time during my whole life, I
was off for the first boat from Heysham to Belfast.

But before leaving the Academy I made a discovery. Some
unknown person obviously had doubts about either my illness
or the more serious matter of my claims to conversion. I went

Shamrock

into the lecture hall to collect some things from my desk. Inside it lay a sheet of paper. Two lines of verse were written on it parodying a well-known evangelical chorus,

> *On Christ the solid rock I stand,*
> *All other ground is sham-rock.*

CHAPTER IV

Me and My 'Doppelgänger'

❦❦❦

And I defeated the terror of the Water. How often in my boyhood my mother, worn out with keeping us and exasperated by my bad behaviour, had threatened to leave us by crossing the Water! How wide the Water had seemed then, and how wide too when I had left Ireland for the Bible Academy. Perhaps the blood in generations of American emigrants' veins and of those bound for the hiring fairs of northern England sang sadly in my veins. But the passengers in the old boats going to America seldom returned to Ireland just as the hirelings drifted away to Glasgow and Liverpool. Yet here was I gliding safe and sound up Belfast Lough only a few months after leaving it.

I did not waste time on the city for I had already determined to spend my few weeks of freedom away in the West, in what I regarded as home, the whitewashed farmhouse tucked away between Fermanagh's lakes and hills. This had been the last of my billets as an evacuee. And with the ageing farmer Christy, and his sister Maggie, who surrounded my young life with love, I found not only a home but my own self. From the first moments, Christy and Maggie had regarded me as the son of the house. The tiny room with its white-painted bed off the kitchen was mine—the Cub's.

At every crisis in my adolescent life, and there had already been many, I went back to the farm to draw new strength out of its serenity.

I had taken my fill of Bible Academies for a while. Without a thought I got off the ship and went to Belfast Station for the first train going to Enniskillen.

Behind the farmhouse door there was a yellow curtain to cover up my dark preaching clothes. At the back of the great open turf fire with its tangle of adjustable pot-hangers and chains on the crane, amongst the bread-irons and trivets, the rabbit skins and goose wings, were my old farm socks. Within an hour of arriving I had my leggings and hobnailed boots on and had gone into the hills with traps and snares.

And just as the Bible Academy looked for tokens of the Lord's seal, I wanted 'showers of blessing' on my Fermanagh stay. Every bog-bank, each spring-water sheugh, a dozen bends of the Scillies river, the views of the seven lakes from the fort hill, our own heron pools, each field of barley stubble, the flax hill, the desolate winter meadows where goldcrests gleaned among the blackheads, the pine plantations ready for cutting, the great hedges of the fort which gave shelter to the out-wintering bullocks, every treacherous hole in the cow-pass glazed with ice, each badger sett, every fighting pike, the bat caves, the ragged profile of Mount Belmore, all these and a thousand and one other wonders were waiting for me—the Cub come home.

My fishing lines still lived in the barn with the best horse-trap, and the only repair necessary was to an odd snare peg or two. And that very night farm history was made. Soon after dark I set a trap down by the bog and before the fire was raked for the night a dog fox had been caught. But by morning in the same trap on the same run the vixen was bagged.

When Christy and I came down from the fort it was not yet first milking. We made our way across the water-meadows and through our own secret tunnels in the elder thickets, and so up into the bog where we discovered the miracle of the second fox. It was still dark and the amber halo thrown out by the hurricane lamp fell on the struggling vixen. As I carried the still-warm body into the fir plantation for skinning, I realized I was happier and even prouder than ever I was taking the suit-case with all its Bibles sold back to the Academy. I could not help trying to guess what Sister Winifred's comment would have been had she seen her favourite protégé confirming the fox's sex and then ripping the carcase open to see if it was with young.

For a whole month I had no cares about what anybody thought or said, except for our neighbours who gathered around the fire for a *ceili* and sing-song in the evenings. For a month I listened to old country tales. No idea came into my head that I should preach or adopt an attitude in front of these people, who were my old friends. It no longer mattered that Red Hughie had stolen the tea urn from the Methodist preaching house to make a poteen still up in the mountains. With none to hinder them, the Free State woodmen came in and sang their haunting rebel songs between the dancing and the blaring out of Orange ballads. For a whole month I did not hunger for my Daily Bread notes, nor did I look at the current Geneva portion.

How to adjust the plough to the lie of the far hill became a nobler thing than prating in pulpits. I was happier to be feeding up the stirks with linseed-cake before the fair, than I would have been facing a new congregation. Talk of mixing clovers and rye-grass seemed sweeter to me than threshing about in Thessalonians or effusing over Galatians. Many of the stirks I was dealing with now I had helped into the world. Every field that was broken now, I had watched sown and reaped. I had helped to cart each harvest home to the warm, dusty hay-loft. When I was an evacuee, hardly with the dust of city bricks and mortar shaken off my feet, the well-stacked hay-loft had seemed the most romantic place imaginable.

Not only had I gone there to find nests made by the hens, but also to seek the nests made by lovers from the nearby Orange hall. Whenever a dance had been held in the hall, our hay-loft was a recognized place for amorous operations which may or may not have concluded with actual seduction. And I would wait to see which of my favourite friends were being taken away towards the hay-loft so that next day I could go and roll naked in the same hay-cradle, creating as I did an imaginary romance, longing at the same time for the day when it would no longer be imaginary.

Returning again after my great experience of the world, gained by crossing the Water, my evacuee years seemed to have happened aeons previously. In fact, only four years had passed since I had been evacuated from Belfast soon after the war began. I was twelve then. Now I was bordering on seventeen. Christy's pikes of hay were as carefully dressed as ever. The beam-high beds of corn and barley were as warm and spider-ridden. But gone was the desire to play with my own body. Bute Street had cured me of that.

Also, something had gone from the farm's magnetism over me. Perhaps the quickening pulse of adolescence and the glimpse of a wide world which the American liberty ships had given me were responsible for a new, questing restlessness. Although I loved the place still, very quickly I was not content to cross the old orchard twice a day to fetch water from the spring. I grew impatient of the cattle meandering up the pass for milking. It was not the Bible Academy I missed, but the sense it gave me of being on the threshold of adventure. So at the end of the month Maggie and Christy came out to the head of the long winding lane to wave me yet another good-bye.

I went into Enniskillen with the lad on the creamery lorry. He was known around the district as a topping dancer, but my Anthony Eden hat and horn-rimmed glasses made him nervous. He preferred to be watched slinking through the bog to a secret session in the hay-loft than to be chauffeuring a pompous young evangelist.

For pompous I was. Once away from Maggie's lane and the security of the little white-painted bedroom off the farm-kitchen, once away from the only place in the world where I could be myself, I was quick to re-erect the façade of respectable righteousness. Similar masks were fashionable in my native Belfast and few, if any, would notice that it was false. Mine never shone brighter with holiness than when I was in my home town.

My religious respectability had no other choice. It had to

shine. So many other people now expected it to. I had reached the stage of being afraid to let my hair down under the soul-greedy eyes of the evangelical group who had 'saved' me, the other group which had witnessed my 'Second Blessing', the others who had encouraged me to accept 'the Call' to the mission-field, and those who had lined my pockets with hard cash 'by faith'. In addition, and perhaps this worried me more than the others, my family's eyes rested on me.

Big 'Ina, my mother, and my sisters must not see so much as a spot of tarnish on my heavenly armour. This armour had supposedly carried me far above the place of my old life. Beneath me now were the racing-pigeon lofts and billiard-halls of the mean streets which had been home for the first twelve years of my life. Before going back to Wales again I dearly wanted to see Big 'Ina. A bond existed between us which had rarely found expression.

During childhood, while my sisters slept, I was the one who lay awake terrified lest Big 'Ina's weary footsteps should fail to sound in the street as she came home from a pre-dawn stoking of school boilers. Late at night, I stood waiting for her to come back from cleaning offices and classrooms. I knew the boiler fumes and the dust irritated her weak chest causing the 'ship-yard bark' which terrified me. Too often I had seen her name on the danger list at the Royal Victoria Hospital.

As I went towards my old home it struck me as odd that I should already, with comparatively little effort, be safe from the clutches of the poverty which had threatened to drag us all down. I resented the city because of the burden and hardship with which it had crushed my mother after my father's accident. She had been left without even the few shillings of a widow's pension. Big 'Ina worked from early morning to late at night to try and save us from orphanages. Remembering this made me want to see her all the more. I hated having to be pompous, yet even she would expect it now that I was well and truly 'saved'. She knew, as I did, that I could not join her and her boy-friend down the Pass in a glass of porter.

Nevertheless, I went home, hurrying by the houses where I

had gone from door to door for so many years with my parish-orphan pin-hole card, hoping for the pennies which were the only 'charity' given my mother to support us. Now that I was dressed to the nines in my preacher clothes, I was afraid of being stopped by the kind woman two doors from us who had always saved her newspapers for use in our lavatory, or the butcher who used to keep the late Saturday night scraps for us. How I had hated charity as a boy. Having risen above it now, I wanted everyone else to do the same, but especially Big 'Ina.

I walked down the back entry to the house. Mine was as bogus a respectability as that of the parlours at the front, those rooms which were as unreal as the paper flowers set by the windows or the plaster casts of the Cherry Boy. In our street the only ones who lived in the parlours were the dead. Their stiffness admirably matched the stiffness of horsehair sofas. The living only went into the parlours to use the penny-in-the-slot gas meters, and how many of those had I not forced? Little wonder that I now went furtively down the entry, rather like my mother's lovers, so that I should not be seen by the rector, the Orphan Society Secretary or the neighbours.

Nobody was at home. But I shinned over the backyard wall, not caring for the moment whether my preaching clothes suffered in the process. I got into the kitchen, the room where our sort of people lived, the room where the lodgers coming in from the coalyards would wash in the iron tub in front of the fire, where everyone was reminded not to wet the seat going up the yard.

Big 'Ina came in at last. Although she was tired and ill-looking there was still that animal beauty about her which made the corner-boys whistle and the engine-drivers on the railway behind the house blow their whistles. Within my black preacher-dressed breast a pride welled up that I had been born of this woman and her wild drunken man whom fate had cheated by making him a window-cleaner instead of a musician. I could never love people like Sister Winifred as I could this still-beautiful mother, whose beauty had all my own weaknesses.

Yet for every minute of that visit I was ill at ease. I was

afraid the lodgers would come in and call me Bobbie instead of
my 'saved' Robert and ask if I was 'courtin' strong'. And there
was the possibility of meeting Harry, Big 'Ina's 'steady',
coming in with half-a-dozen Guinnesses and a wrapping of
whelks. It disturbed me that the time dragged. I fled for the
evening boat with my umbrella and hat before anybody should
appear who might puncture my religious pomposity.

But none of them knew, nobody but myself knew, that my
newly-acquired grandeur was not more nor less to me than a
skeleton key. I had to use it to unlock the door to the world
beyond Belfast and the shipyard—a world I was determined to
have. I wanted to get on in life. One person, however, did see,
not chinks, but large and alarming cracks in my spiritual
armour. This was the Vice-Principal.

He saw that something was wrong. He probably did not
understand what. But his instincts were roused. And he
showed me this soon after my return from Ireland. At Christmas Sister Winifred had shown her special favour by giving me
a scriptural autograph book. The Vice-Principal had now taken
it away to sign. When I got it back again, instead of the usual
Biblical verse in Hebrew or Greek I found lines which clearly
showed the man's feeling towards me,

> *If in vision fair, you could but see*
> *The man the Saviour meant,*
> *Then never more would you be,*
> *The man you are, content.*

Glow brightly in the pulpit I might, but nothing could hide
from the Vice-Principal's eyes the underlying fact that I was
not a good student. He worried himself about the amount of
time I devoted to dressing the Bible depot's windows. He
failed to understand how I could go off for days at a time, supposedly hawking Bibles among the ships. Being also our senior
lecturer in English, the Vice-Principal criticized my essays. His
remarks, however, were not conerned with the nice turning of
a literary phrase but with theological 'soundness'. My essays,
every one of them, he said, lacked 'scriptural surety'. My mind,

he said, was on the world and not on the Book. I was pre-occupied with musing about Ireland instead of with demonstrations concerning pre-millennial truth. My thoughts turned obstinately towards that Belfast house shaken day and night by passing trains. No act of will could blot from my mind the want which had blighted my early years.

Could I really be blamed if when asked to write on the 'Salutations in the market-place', I did not see the Biblical scribes in their 'long clothing' nor hear their exchanges in Hebrew? The word 'market-place' brought the jargon of Belfast's Friday markets to my ears. And how was I to convey the strange meaning and harmony of these things to the Vice-Principal? He would not know, as I did by experience, of the human vultures who waited for the market doors to close so that we could gorge on hot peas drowned by the vinegar shaker and spill the day's cracked eggs into bottles. In the Vice-Principal's view I was wrong to see my boyhood self in shop yards sieving through sawdust barrels for forgotten grapes. He would have been happier if my pen had pelted the scribes with beery plums and blackened bananas. I was, in short, not ashamed of my 'worldly days', and not to be ashamed of them was a sin.

I knew inwardly that there was nothing to be done. In my heart I had already forsaken the Bible Academy. It simply remained now for matters to come to a head, which they did soon enough.

When the Vice-Principal next stood on the lecture rostrum I was, as usual, absent, gorging myself on the flesh-pots of the American liberty ships. The Vice-Principal must have observed my absence though he made no comment. But he did inquire as to the whereabouts of a certain girl student who normally sat under his lectern. He hated her. Her gentleness, her sincerity, her humility, cut deeply into his own bombastic, Cambridge-donnishness, undermining his professional holiness.

This girl spoke neither with the tongues of men nor of angels. Her quiet and at times almost inaudible voice was an offence to the Vice-Principal, and he bullied her on every possible occasion. Well might he bellow and roar and expect us to do the same if pagan Africa was to be converted and the trams swinging down Bute Street were to be filled with volleys of divine praise. But the Vice-Principal failed to see that the divine scheme of things might have use also for small, still voices.

Sympathy, however, was forthcoming for this mouse of a girl who had a lion's heart. All the students objected to the Vice-Principal's description of her as an 'inmate'. 'Where's the inmate?' he shouted angrily at the beginning of that fateful lecture. All those present in the lecture hall understood whom he meant. The girl's awkwardness and shyness often gave the impression that she was a mental case. But it was cruel of the Vice-Principal to imply that she was or ought to be an 'inmate' of a lunatic asylum. The students were outraged and composed a letter protesting to the man and demanding an apology.

When I returned from the docks I was asked to add my signature to that of the others. The letter was then handed to the Vice-Principal. We sat back and waited. But not for long. His anger exploded, and the result was an extraordinary meeting of staff and students which lasted at boiling point until even the evil hour of ten o'clock had slipped by unnoticed. In his specially donned clerical garb the Vice-Principal shouted and raved and his face was like an apoplectic beetroot, and well might the ladies upstairs be on their knees praying against a heart attack.

There *was* an attack, but on me. The Vice-Principal used me as a scapegoat. Two terms of pent-up dislike burst out. I was an 'Irish puppy' and was undoubtedly behind all this trouble. He left no doubt in anybody's mind that so far as he was concerned, I was the worm eating the Academy's rose heart.

From that night, the Academy was split in twain. The two factions could not find any charity of heart. Despite the Vice-Principal's determination to destroy me, I nevertheless continued to enjoy the protective custody of the Principal and Sister Winifred, and to the annoyance of certain students, continued to eat in their private dining-room. But I was thought to be outgrowing my spiritual strength and therefore in need of careful nurturing. Also, my soul's health was endangered by a hankering, which I could not resist, after High Churchmanship.

This was no more than a mere flirtation, a desire for change. If the Academy people had left me alone I would probably soon have tired of High Church antics. However, the Academy's prohibition on things like vestments and sanctuary bells only drove me to find out more about it. And in a place like the Academy such fellow-travelling could not remain secret.

I was found out in my errors the day when the Principal came back from visiting Sully sanatorium, his special preserve. As though announcing the date for the end of the world the Principal said that some Roman Catholic nuns had been seen in the wards talking to patients. A lengthy prayer orgy was immediately called for in the Academy to rectify the matter. Students and staff were expected to attend. I had seen such marathons before, and knew that I could not escape for at least several hours. Partly from boredom and partly from annoyance at the anti-Rome campaign to which, had I been God, I should not have listened, I shut my eyes and eventually fell asleep. Not until Sister Winifred began bellowing out a hymn, thereby not only waking me but nearly blasting me out of my chair, did I discover that with the sole exception of myself all those present had taken up the arms of prayer against Rome. My silence was interpreted as sympathy with Roman Catholicism rather than as annoyance at the narrow pettiness of my brothers and sisters in the Academy.

Next morning every student was given a copy of *Guilty Clergy* by Percival Petter. And it was whispered in my ear that although I had received the 'Second Blessing' of the Holy Ghost after conversion I had not yet passed through the waters of baptism. Apparently, my perfectly straightforward, ordinary christening as a baby in St. Patrick's, the church which dominated the Belfast docks, was no good. It just would not do. The protest I registered about this was completely ignored, though I was quite excited when they obtained the use of a Plymouth Brethren hall. The great tank of water was warmed

up and I was duly lowered into it securely fastened in the
Principal's arms and accompanied by the ringing of hallelujahs. The only effect of my enforced baptism I can remember
clearly is being annoyed that a perfectly good suit had been
ruined in the soaking.

In their efforts to eliminate human mediation between a man
and his God, the Plymouth Brethren, as a sect, disposed of such
fallible creatures as priests or ministers. However, to avoid
the troubles which arise when the blind lead the blind, they
instituted Bible teachers and writers. These gentlemen 'lived by
faith' and ministered at the 'Breaking of Bread' and special
missions by appointment only. One such teacher, a man of no
little renown, was imported into the Academy to deal with my
straying. He promptly whisked me off to his home for a week,
to make sure that I was well and truly anchored in that water-
tight sect.

Naturally, I enjoyed being the centre of attention and controversy once again. I found it pleasant to pass my mornings in a
warm study sipping herbal coffee while the Great Bible Teacher
fed me on the 'milk of the Word'. Unhappily, I was thinking all
the time of the heavenly smell escaping from the kitchen. But
tempting and wholesome though those dishes prepared
especially for me might have been, they were not the spicy
food of Bute Street. I began to hunger for the dockland life.

While staying at the house my afternoons were free.
Luncheon was eaten to the sound of my host's and hostess's
suggestions that I go out and walk on the green hills and fill my
young lungs with God's health-giving air. I agreed that, yes, it
was a good idea and that I would go out as soon as the meal
was over. I did, but went straight back into Cardiff and to
Tiger Bay. Danish laughter, Greek kebabs, Moglai curries,
sweaty bodies, moll stories, Yankee messrooms were all
spread out before me, awaiting me with sanguine life, and,
strangely, with beauty as Fermanagh's hills waited. And after
the big thrill, after the last pint of bitter, and when the Central
Station loomed up to speed me home, I fell into a feeling of
chaos. Louis MacNeice put it,

Me and My 'Doppelgänger'

After the legshows and the brandies
And all the pick-me-ups for tired
Men there is a feeling
Something more is required.

The strain of trying to balance the serious intentions to snare my soul in a heavenly net with my own taste for Bute Town was overshadowed by a greater strain. At the other end of the rope, Rome joined the tug-o'-war for my soul. Or rather, I trailed after the Scarlet Woman. The puff of incense caught in a stray sunbeam through the parish church's dusty window had turned out to be a cloud on a bigger horizon. And I found the embrace of the Scarlet Woman more exciting than the coconut-smelling, mahogany arms of Cardiff's dolly-dives.

Rome's attraction lay only partly in religion. The Scarlet Woman's charms resided to a considerable extent in the fact that for most of my life they had been forbidden fruit. Reared in pre-war Belfast in the Protestant sector, Roman Catholicism had been shown to me as the world's greatest evil, and Catholics our greatest enemy, Germans not excluded. Indeed while a boy I blamed the war on Hitler and the Pope. It was undeniable that the Pope had put a curse on Prussia when Bismark proscribed the Jesuits. Yet in spite of this, Germany became powerful and swamped Austria and France. Success was short-lived for when the Roman Catholic Central Party voted Hitler into power, Germany was doomed. A burning curiosity about such vile wickedness was, of course, the inevitable consequence.

A childhood impregnated with anti-Catholic Orange-brand patriotism was not easily sloughed off. Even in those days I soon discovered that some of our ideas about Catholics were no more true than was Father Christmas. And later, in Fermanagh, I found that the parish priest was as welcome to Maggie's Rhode Island Reds for his table as were the Catholic herdsmen to our spring well. All that I cared then, was that the Fenian farmboys who came across the Border were good wildfowlers and singers.

67

However, in school they forced us to learn a miserable catechism called *How We Differ from Rome*. I had not wanted to differ from Rome then, for that would have destroyed the idyll. And now, as a black-suited Bible student, I did not wish particularly to differ from Rome. My preacher's clothes were the uniform of prejudice and fear. And I hated the Belfast people who had turned my inborn religious sense into a proprietary brand of evangelical cant. I hated the Bible Academy for patronizing me and trying to force me into a strait-jacket of soul-saving respectability. I hated myself for being so easily persuaded to forget the shining freedom from being afraid which I had once known at Maggie's farm.

The effect of this was not to drive me away from religion altogether, but to send me flying off to find out more about those demon-possessed people whom I had been brought up to hate and was now expected to hate professionally—Roman Catholics.

While I was yet eating and breaking bread in the house of Great Bible Teacher, while he was still expounding scriptural profundities of inconceivable tedium, I found a fascinating junk-shop down town. Amongst the mummified-looking cats asleep in its window, amongst *A Present from Brighton* cups and the chipped remains of willow pattern dinner services, amongst its brass candlesticks and Oxford-framed texts, lay a crucifix. It was old and made of wood into which worms had bored irreligiously, and which many devout fingers had polished during the years until it looked as smooth as a sea-ground pebble. But sufficient remained of the impaled Christ to see that the carver had made Him in the form of a Greek athlete, so that the unpainted torso and limbs were in the full vigour of manhood, until they were hung on a gallows. And somehow that young, tortured Jesus was different from the rather prating one conjured up by the Bible Academy.

I went in and bought Him, and took Him home in my colportage suitcase.

Unluckily, and, I suppose, inevitably, my crucifix was seen by other students and I became embroiled in a bitter argument about Catholicism. Then I was summoned to the Principal's study. After a long harangue, to which I listened only enough to gather that he thought my crime worse than I had regarded Abraham's smoking the Apples of Gold, the Principal took my crucifix, broke it in half over his knee, and threw the two pieces in the fire.

The Principal's vandalism decided me. I would definitely find out about the Roman Church for myself. This was solely on a scientific, fact-finding basis with no plans on my part for becoming a Catholic. I simply wanted to know whether the accusations against them I heard every day now in lectures were as untrue as those I had heard in childhood.

On my next visit to Cardiff, I went straight to Newport Road. Here, on a modest house a small plate announced that the Archbishop of Cardiff lived there. I knocked and was admitted and found myself in a hallway as bare as the Academy's. Somehow I had expected the unseemly luxury of wealth extorted from the terrified faithful. Humble was hardly the word to describe the Archbishop's house. And when I was shown in, a gentle Irishman greeted me, a man who might have been talking about the price of bullocks at the fair instead of the Immaculate Conception. I felt completely at home. As the Archbishop pushed a pinch of snuff up one nostril he might have been any one among a score of Fermanagh farm-folk whom I remembered gathered round Maggie's fire for an evening *ceili*. I could imagine him broadcasting corn from an old sack apron, or building a stack of barley on stone-straddles.

The little house and its occupant so enchanted me that some time passed before I realized that my wet umbrella was causing a stream to run across the linoleum like an untrained puppy. Covert glances at my companion showed that he had not noticed the stream on his floor. I liked that. Maggie and Christy would not have minded either. And the Archbishop's simple delight in having me to talk to could have been the same also.

It gave me a secret satisfaction to know that neither Sister Winifred nor the Principal would have approved of my umbrella making puddles on the carpets of their private apartments. But Dr. McGrath understood me. And when he learnt that I came from within the Bible Academy's hallowed walls, to my surprise he raised no eyebrows nor said a word against the place or the people or their precepts. And neither then nor at any subsequent meetings did he attempt any persuasion to make me Catholic. He put himself at my disposal and answered questions. Indeed, at times he seemed almost reluctant to talk about religion and instead chatted about Ireland or gave me lists of places in Wales which I should visit.

Meanwhile weeks grew into months. Allied armies poured across France, flooding the Netherlands, and inundating the Rhine's banks, and then it was V-E Day. My *doppelgänger* which haunted Bute Town now had a new, secret companion who frequented the hills of Rome. Yet, in spite of such a multi-level existence I remained firmly in position as the apple of Sister Winifred's eye. Even the Principal, perhaps in a mood of conciliation after consigning my crucifix to an *auto-da-fé*, had given me a new and bigger Bible, inscribed 'With affection and thanks for services rendered to the Bible House'. And I was still building a reputation as a preacher, feeding vanity with vanity.

The Academy celebrated V-E Day by putting a coloured photograph of Field-Marshal Montgomery in the Bible depot's window. The Field-Marshal was considered to a 'sound' Christian, though, of course, not so sound as General Dobbie, who delighted in the evangelical platform. Indeed, his book *Very Present Help*, was our shop's best-seller.

My own personal V-E victory was in bagging the pulpit of the big Baptist church up the road which did not usually select its preachers from the Academy. And not only was this engagement for their V-E Sunday but also for their church anniversary which happily coincided. My name went up outside on the noticeboard in really large letters. They were hardly large enough, however, to satisfy my vanity. No actress took more pleasure in showing admirers her name in bright West End lights than I had in leading my American sailors past the Baptist church. For the first day or so my pride was admingled with vexation. The poster artist had spelt my name wrongly. I had to buy a pot of blue poster paint and steal up to rectify matters after dark.

Anyway, V-E Sunday went off without a hitch, and for once there were some dividends for all the spiritual investment, for my sermon led one young man to follow me into training for the ministry. The service had a suitable military flavour. An A.T.S. officer read the first lesson and Hal, a young Billy Budd type of American sailor, read the second lesson from the New Testament. I can hardly believe that today Hal is wielding the big Bible 'with power' in his native Ohio, for he had more than a glimpse of my other life down Bute Street.

The European war was over and so was spring for it was giving way to a heady summer. Blackcap and warblers came to rouse the woods outside the city, and the jubilant trills of wrens penetrated the underwoods. Tinkerbell was getting fat again on red clover. Pennywort was pushing through the cracks of the stone bridge leading to the evergreen world of the docks.

Once again, I began to look for preaching engagements which would take me out of the city at week-ends. Sister Edna was a favourite speaker (and still is) and she sometimes asked me to go and share engagements. And in her company I went to the towns of the Rhondda. After preaching we walked through the mining streets up to wonderful hills and moors. We took our lunch by rippling trout streams. We stood amazed before fold after fold of valleys vanishing between rounded hills.

To another part of the Rhondda, however, I first went with Sister Winifred, and this was not so beautiful. The House O' The Trees at Penygraig was an Approved Probation Home for teenage boys. It was difficult to preach there for the place made me feel both sad and a hypocrite for doing so. Most of the youths shut up there had done things no worse than I had done a few years previously in Belfast. Being on the staff side, rather than the boys', made me uncomfortable. I had avoided their fate only by the prodigious efforts of the few who had not despaired of me. At The House O' The Trees I could not even be one with boys working down on the farm or in the carpenter's shop. All I could do was sit on the mountainside feeling helpless.

For most week-ends I tried to get preaching engagements which would lead me away to my beloved Brecknockshire properly. Sleeping in the hill farms of the Black Mountains and exploring the Beacons was like being an evacuee all over again discovering land and sky and horizons of no limit, and all those lovely streams, the Senni, the Honddu and Tarell and the lyrical parent rivers of Wye and Usk. And I found Llangorse Lake with all its wildfowl and teeming roach and lurking eels. I explored the untamed majesty clinging about Llangatwg and Llangynidr mountains as they lost their indentity in the encroaching Beacons.

During the week I was restless, feeling stifled by the stale town air. The week-ends could not come fast enough. Sister Winifred used to stand at her upstairs dining-room window which overlooked the square and every road leading into it. When she waved me good-bye on those week-end engagements I could feel her narrowed, sharp eyes following me 'every step of the journey'—a phrase she used when beseeching the Lord to give me 'journeying mercies'.

Be sure your sins will find you out was a favourite maxim at the Academy. And I was sure the all-seeing eyes of God often borrowed Sister Winifred's thick lenses to catch up with me at week-ends. I was soon found out. The Lord's Day Observance was naturally one of the Academy's major causes. Even when preaching 'the Word' all Sunday travel had to be limited to cycling or walking. But in spite of such pious restrictions I often made my way back to Cardiff at Sunday's end to spend the night aboard ship or in a club. Unfortunately, I got myself involved in a brawl one such night, which decorated me with a black eye and a broken nose.

In itself, this was not serious. I had known black eyes and bent noses before, but on previous occasions I had not been a practising evangelist. Quite clearly, I would have to steer clear of the Academy for at least a week. But where to go in the

Me and My 'Doppelgänger'

meantime was quite a problem. And so I came back to the Black Mountains and without much difficulty found Abraham. He was living in the steading of a deserted cottage. The odd thing about this was that Sister Edna had first taken me out to this cottage while I was on the previous summer's mission. But at that time an old woman had still been living in the little stone house whom Sister Edna and I used to visit. At each visit Sister Edna collected a great bundle of sticks for the old woman's fire and carried them to the cottage in her cape. To see the cottage now deserted and already showing the first signs of dereliction sent a chill through me.

Abraham's occupation of the steading was better than nothing, however, though I doubt whether it was a way of life which Sister Edna would have cared for. I could not go up to her farm now and talk about Abraham for she would have wondered why he did not come also to have a bath like all the caravan missioners. And it would have been difficult for me to explain why Abraham was forced to live wild in the mountains. How could I say why he could not, like myself, visit Sister Edna when she stayed on the coast at Penarth with her family in a large house whose doors were thrown wide to me and to all the American sailors I cared to take home?

Apart from the ingrained grime in Abraham's skin, Sister Edna would also probably not have approved of Abraham calling Solomon's seal by its old name, 'sow's tits'. But he did call it this because he used sow's tits for curing my black eye. Abraham was as good a doctor as he was poacher. Within an hour of meeting him he had been to the woods and had a colony of Solomon's seal beaten into an ointment. My bruises disappeared in a day or two under the influence of this leaf balm.

I had seen Abraham several times since the summer and now that the war was over he returned to do odd jobs on a farm, a place where I could easily contact him. But Abraham saw no advantage in being a cog in the comparatively simple machine of farm life. Things like insurance cards and ration books and set working hours frightened and disgusted him. He would not be tied down. Nevertheless, he was not a 'son of rest' and only

73

went on tramp rounds to get 'freeman's pick-ups' as he called cigarette butts. Something wild and free in him would not be caught. He preferred to live in the hills than in dockland bumdives. And because he lived in the hills I sought Abraham's company. I considered that what he did not know about birds was not worth knowing. His mimicry of birdsongs was marvellous. It had a literal imitation which Messiaen could never have orchestrated. His lark-like trilling would have shamed the violins of Haydn's quartet. Nettle-beds and hedgerows would have awaited the arrow-flight of whitethroat on hearing his vigorous warbling and coarse scolding. The irony was that lark or whitethroat might well have ended their brief lives in Abraham's pot.

But this revealed only one side of Abraham. He was not a man who put much store by words and talking, and I only heard him use the Romany tongue once, and that was when we became 'brothers'. I felt honoured and intrigued all at once when he suggested this, for I had always fancied myself as being part gypsy from a great-grandmother. As the evangelicals insisted on the 'Blood of the Lamb' being so essential to salvation, and the Children of Israel had needed the blood of a 'red heifer without spot' to sprinkle before the tabernacle of the congregation, so Abraham insisted on pricking both our left wrists. Then he tied them together with a rush band not unlike the one which Maggie in Fermanagh had been given to wear as a charm when she broke her wrist. After my blood had mingled sufficiently with Abraham's, a solemn pronouncement, again like a charmer's, was said in Romany. Henceforth, I belonged to the 'black blood people' of the road.

And so, the first post-war summer term rushed by, devouring the wonderful mountain week-ends one by one. In the wake of memories left behind my fondest ones were of Monica. She had come to help out in the Bible shop, so that I was in and out every five minutes. But I was not in love with her. She was so beautiful, so understanding that I could not bear to see her destined for a damp manse in the Highlands with Brother Stephen. And, looking back now, I think I did save her. At least I may have helped to unblinker her eyes. Eventually she scandalized everybody by marrying an actor. But before this consummation Monica spent many of her evenings with me. We wandered along the coast locked in dreams of the future and never of the present night air stirring the guelder rose, brushing our hot young bodies.

Now that the war was over, night no longer meant darkness. Lights shone across the bay again. Sister Winifred had all the black-out curtains boiled for days in the great copper to remove their dye. A yellow ball of light fell over the roofless urinal in the square used by the wine-bibbers coming out of the Conservative Club. But nowhere light held such mystery as along the millpond waters of the bay.

Creeks and inlets of twilight shadow streaked the water when Monica and I began our homeward journey for mud cocoa. The town's lights glimmered twice, once from the dusky shore and again in the water's reflection. A complete world showed in the still water, an indigo outline of hills, bars of gold-lined cloud on the first points of fire burning in the depths overhead. The bay's streams of molten gold now paled and hardened into cold blades of steel as the sun went down behind the farthest mountains.

I remember one such evening when Monica and I held hands going home when we saw a large star pendant in the emptiness behind a screen of trees. It flashed icy, crystal colours. The whole sky became velvet, pin-pointed with hosts of stars. Yet we both preferred the land lights. We thought them so romantic, at least, I did for afterwards I wrote:

> *Those were the land lights*
> *Far out on the horizon*
> *Winking to the night*
> *The far endless night.*
>
> *We were on the shore*
> *The warm silent shore,*
> *The lips of the sea caressing and feeling*
> *The breathing, waiting, silent shore.*

Me and My 'Doppelgänger'

We were on the shore
With the birds
And the bone dry stones
Salt dried in the sun of many days.

But there were the lights, the land lights
And there the distant moonscaped clouds massing
Translucent, hollow, empty, real,
Full of holes and ragged openings for the stars
Which are not for men.

The land lights are for men
Travelling by night.

And we were watching them
From the other side of the bay,
Trying to discern their meaning,
Finding their rhythm mysterious
A baffling mystery without answer.

Only the sea knows the answer,
Quietly sleeping.

CHAPTER V

Roman Holiday

❧✿❧

I shared one of the large, uncomfortable double desks in the Acamedy's lecture hall with another student, Brother David. And from the beginning, in some uncanny way, I knew he was going to die tragically. Initially perhaps, it was the strength of this feeling, born of some fey intuition, which drew me towards him. And the Principal also placed us together. I was sixteen years old, and David was not quite eighteen, and we were the Academy's two youngest students.

But at first, I considered my experience of life much wider than David's. He came straight to Wales from his Sussex village. He had never before been on such a journey. He was naïve and sincere and, I thought, was not as fly as myself. He appeared to swallow whole everything dished up by the Academy. And possibly I was sharper than he and had my wits about me so far as life went in this world. But David was different. He lived as a shepherd of the delectable mountains. I could not follow him among those ghostly pastures.

David was a carpenter. His apprenticeship had no doubt helped to develop his fine physique. But the flash of his radiant blue eyes and the pallor of his face came from a different kind of experience. Some of the other students, who came from middle-class suburban backgrounds, often laughed at David's ingenuous manner or at the delight he took in doing his carpentry in the Academy's workshop. Yet nobody laughed when the square workman's hands played a violin. And nobody laughed either when his rather thick Sussex dialect was raised in prayer.

Brother David of the white face and thick mop of black, curly hair was liked by both of the Academy's opposing factions. He had no enemies, and although all were his friends he chose me as special among them. It was his persuasion, for David belonged to the Plymouth Brethren, which had led me to the waters of toal immersion. And through the present crisis of irrevocable disagreement with the Academy, only David's presence had saved me from headlong flight. In return for his friendship and help I brought some of my sailors back for David. Venezuelan or Argentinian ones were the best because he was going as a missionary to South America and wanted to practise Spanish. I could never return all his kindness. I missed more lectures than I attended but nearly always I would find notes inside my desk in David's neat hand. From everybody's point of view, David was the perfect student.

David digressed from rules and regulations only by his inability to remain silent after our ten o'clock curfew. During the first term he came from his room to my Number One. He could not settle to sleep until he knew that I was back safe and sound from my dockland adventures. Since there were only two single rooms for male students and since my own room lay empty so often because of my various jaunts, I agreed to move into David's double room when Brother Edward, being a senior student, wanted to move out from a dormitory. The new arrangement pleased both David and myself very much and we became closer friends than ever.

When my seventeenth birthday came, David was the only student whom I invited to the party which was to be held at Penarth with Sister Edna. I left the Academy for Penarth on the Saturday with some Americans. David was to follow on Monday. The night before I left, a curious thing happened in our bedroom. In the narrow, shadowed room I saw David get up from saying his prayers and slip quickly into bed as usual. But instead of settling to the easy sounds of sleep he sat up suddenly and said he must sing. His voice was rich and sweet.

For an unaccountable reason I was moved then as he sang softly:

> *There's a land that is fairer than day,*
> *And by faith we can see it afar,*
> *For the Father waits over the way,*
> *To prepare us a dwelling-place there.*

I regarded myself as absurd for wanting to cry when he stopped as suddenly as he had begun. Not only would it have shown me to be unmanly (I thought) but it would have destroyed the silence which followed, the silence peculiar to the Bible Academy where there was not even a dog to scratch itself on the bare floorboards, and where not even faulty ball cocks dared to sing in the night.

My birthday Saturday was fine and hot. I enjoyed the afternoon at Penarth. Following the week's usual semi-starvation at the Academy I let myself go at Sister Edna's loaded tables. My day's brightness, however, clouded over every time I looked at Sister Edna. Her benevolence and her desire to please me and make me happy could not hide the fact that she was herself unhappy. I could not guess what had upset her and did not care to ask in case it was some private and perhaps embarrassing matter.

The afternoon wore on and my American friends left before dark to go back to their ships. Then Sister Edna came to me. Her eyes were large with sorrow. What she had been keeping from me was a visit from the Principal and Sister Winifred. They knew how close I had been to David and how our friendship seemed set fair to pull me through my troubles. But David was dead. He had been drowned while swimming that afternoon.

Cuzco, City of the Sun, was once the centre of glory in the Inca empire. It remained so until Spanish fire and sword destroyed it and raised the cross of Rome. From the town of Reading in Berkshire some four centuries later a young Protestant man set out for Peru to take the Roman cross down again. His missionary endeavours were cut short, however, by his untimely death. But in Reading, his dauntless mother prayed that from among the ranks of Rome, yea, even among its priests there might be one seized by the power of the Word and rise up to take her son's place with the Gospel message. And this was precisely what had happened in the extraordinary conversion of Dr. Walter Montano, a nephew of a distinguished President of Bolivia, and, more importantly, a Dominican friar.

The drowned David had been intended for the same needy vineyard in South America. His sudden death left an ugly and noticeable gap in our ranks, and everybody's first thought was how to fill the gap—everybody's thought, that is, except for mine. Although I thought that something terrible would happen to him in this life, David's drowning shocked me. As I folded up his carpenter's apron and packed his violin to send off to his home in Hailsham, in my heart I also packed my own bags.

There was something indecent about the Academy's haste to replace my dead friend. They were disgusting. I could stand them no more. It no longer bothered me that I had nowhere in particular to go. All that mattered was, I intended to go. The Academy people behaved as though God Himself would be unseated if they did not fill the vacancy. Indeed, the Academy people could easily have made me as sick of God as of themselves. But David had prevented such a situation. I saw God in him. About the others, I could not have been less interested. The question was not whether, but when, I should leave the Academy.

My decision was finally settled by the ex-Dominican monk in Inca country. Following closely on David's death I was given a book with a lurid cover. It was *The Monk Who Lived Again*. Dr. Walter Montano, the converted monk, was apparently a great hero among evangelicals, and they referred to him as the Saint Paul of South America. He was also, apparently, living happily with a wife (trained at Moody Bible Institute) in California. Although I was not unmoved by the book's foreword with its touching tale of the Reading mother's prayer for a replacement to carry on her dead boy's work, it did not dispose me favourably towards the ex-friar.

I searched the book diligently but could find no reason which struck me as being a worthwhile one for leaving the monastery. The climax for Dr. Montano came when he saw his fellow monks celebrating his birthday by a party—'and generally gave way to the pranks which wine and good fellowship might suggest'. Well, I certainly could see no harm in this. Had the grim atmosphere of our Academy been relieved by laughter now and then, I might not have been driven to find my own 'good fellowship' elsewhere.

At a time when prayers were still being offered for somebody to go to South America in the place of Brother David (a time, also, when some missionaries were on furlough from Peru and Chile and in attendance at our Convention, where, on hearing of my flirtation with Rome, they joined the throng of those 'up-holding me at the Throne of Grace'), at a time like that, I went out for another talk with the Roman Catholic Archbishop of Cardiff. I told him all about the monk who lived again and about other wildly untrue, or exaggerated Protestant notions about monasteries and convents. We knew each other quite well by now. Not altogether without a twinkle in his eye, the Archbishop suggested that I should find out for myself whether or not I would become a chained prisoner if I got behind a monastery wall.

On the morning after the Convention ended (I could scarcely believe a whole year had passed since the previous one) I caught a train to Bournemouth. Plans had been made for me to stay during the summer vacation at St. Joseph's, a convalescent home run by nuns, so that I could see something of conventual life for myself. An agitated Principal and a distraught Sister Winifred came to the station with me, begging and threatening by turns. But I was adamant, feeling that I was old enough to put their Protestant prejudices to the test. After all, I had retained some native intelligence in spite of a year's influence of the Academy.

Nobody needed to tell me that the cheap trash about convents, bought in sex-magazine shops and devoured by the 'elect', was nonsense. You had only to read in such books about nuns fleeing over convent walls or of the babies nuns conceived by priests being destroyed in quicklime pits, to see that nine times out of ten there was not even a basis of truth in such tales.

Nevertheless, lingering doubts remained in my mind and they had to be pulled out like a rotten tooth stump. The effects of a strict Protestant upbringing and an education consisting to no small extent of anti-Roman Catholic propaganda, were difficult to be rid of.

The first thing to catch my eye in St. Joseph's when I arrived, pleased with the mildness of balmy Bournemouth, was a photograph of the Queen, the present Queen Mother. She had been framed and hung beside a statue of the patron saint. This countered everything in my early upbringing. I had become a member of a junior Orange Lodge at the age of ten. I learnt that one of the 'Twenty Reasons For Being an Orangeman' was 'Because Popery maintains a continual rancour against the Protestant people of Great Britain, receiving their charities with ingratitude, and stimulating its followers to detest the "Saxon", and to loathe the rule and realm of England!' The gable walls on *our* Protestant side of Belfast's Blackstaff river bore such painted signs as 'To Hell with the Pope'. And *their* gables, on the little river's farther side were decorated with exactly opposing sentiments. Never the twain met—until I walked into St. Joseph's entrance hall.

A smiling nun took my bag and led me inside, and she, like many of the others, was Irish. I never heard them mention anything about politics the whole time I stayed there with them. But they had not forgotten Ireland. At concerts for St. Joseph's patients they asked me to sing *Down by the Sally Gardens* and *The Ballynure Ballad*.

Where were the quicklime pits? Where were the 'inquisitorial instruments of the Dominicans' which appeared in the book about Dr. Montano? Why did St. Joseph's nuns not dance and drink together on feast days, or crawl on the floor, or kneel on peach stones when they were doing penance? Perhaps a good reason was that the nuns were too busy. The running of a large convalescent home left little time for the painting of a Virgin's face to represent her in a good or bad mood. Running about after ill people left little energy, and lights were doused at quite as respectable an hour as the Bible Academy's. In vain I looked from my bedroom window over sleeping Bournemouth roofs to find signs of immoral night traffic.

The convent disappointed me. If only I could have found one example of monstrous behaviour to prove that my Protestant prejudices were at least partly justified, it would have made my way ahead clearer. But there was nothing. The only commotion I heard was early one morning. And when I slipped downstairs to see what was afoot, all I found was old Sister Frances noisily scrubbing the long passages. Sister Frances became a good friend and insisted on my spending Christmas at St. Joseph's because her family in County Tyrone were fattening up good Ulster turkeys for the convent.

I liked Bournemouth. I had not yet assumed grand airs which would make me sneer at the town's *élite* as did Karen Blixen, the Danish authoress. For the first time in my adolescence I was leading something approaching a normal life. The patients were mostly working-class boys and men from all over England, sent south to enjoy the pine-scented gentleness of Bournemouth. A young plumber's mate from Coventry, called Ted, often went with me to tea dances at the Pavilion. I could also go into pubs quite openly without fear of either being seen or of embarrassing scenes afterwards.

The part of my convent life which influenced me most, however, was the contact with families whose sons served at Mass in the convent chapel when they came home from public school or university. One family in particular interested me for it was headed by one of the most wonderful women I had met since leaving Maggie in Fermanagh. Henrietta Ormonde-Masterson was, or at least seemed, old to my seventeen years. But it made no difference. When she began her endless flow of Irish stories, the richness of her voice and the breadth of her human understanding made me adore her. She was also the only person I ever knew who displayed the Irish Republic's tricolour at the foot of her Lady of Lourdes statue. With a hint of self-mocking in her lilting voice she told me that, of course, she had only put the flag there because her friend Lady Sherston-Baker had a Union Jack under *her* Madonna.

A curious coincidence gave Mrs. Ormonde-Masterson and me common ground for conversation. Dr. McManaway, Bishop of Clogher, had confirmed me in the Church of Ireland. But Henrietta could hardly believe her ears. Did young Jamie MacManaway *really* become a bishop, she asked, her eyebrows raised. The last she saw of him was when he was being driven from their garden gate by her father for making overtures to the young, much too young, Henrietta.

Ecclesiastical dignity as represented by the Bishop's great bulk was not lessened by the pirate's black patch which he wore over one eye. But what fear he put into me when I was an evacuee in his country diocese. One day he stopped on the road and asked me my name and the address of my billet for he caught me pulling the girls' dresses up. For nights I lay in bed terrified lest he should write to our Bishop in Belfast and put to an end the five shillings a week church orphan fund which supported me. When the Bishop of Clogher appeared a year later and talked with the confirmation candidates to find out if indeed they were fit and prepared for the great sacrament, even then I felt sure that the one dim eye would focus on me and warn me against the dangers of trying to discover the colour of the girls' underwear.

I could scarcely credit now, that this Bishop and Henrietta's young admirer were one and the same person. But they were, and I had no reason to suspect Mrs. Ormonde-Masterson of embroidering the truth. She was not a prude or priggish in the slightest way and I thought how Sister Winifred would have curled at the edges like a frost-touched leaf at my new friend's forthrightness.

It was difficult for me to accustom myself to the fact that

Henrietta's Bournemouth house was an open one for many famous Jesuit priests. Even now, in my inner Protestant soul, I found it faintly disturbing though I enjoyed myself. Perhaps no name, Dublin, Falls Road, Maynooth, Rome or De Valera (whom we burnt every year in effigy) struck such terror in our young Protestant hearts as the name 'Jesuit' had done. Hitler's spy service was milk-mild in comparison and we had the written Orange word, 'Jesuits are openly tolerated in Great Britain and Ireland, contrary to the express laws of the Empire'.

Many of Henrietta's Jesuits were converts to Catholicism, and I eventually went to see them at the Sacred Heart presbytery. Not one made the slightest move to rush me into conditional baptism. There was no attempt to snatch me away from the Bible Academy. I went simply to get straight regarding my prejudices, over which they were all most patient. Weeks went by and still there was no whisper that I should in my way be forced to seek admission to the Roman Catholic Church. I was curious and they were not going to take advantage of mere curiosity. So much could not be said for the Bible Academy's indecent haste in accepting me when I made an enquiry from Belfast.

There were, of course, some people praying that I might find grace to enter the church. Among them was a convert of ninety. Mrs. More-Molyneux lived at Farnham in Surrey and asked me on a long visit. I saw no reason why not and so promptly exchanged the cucumber sandwich tea-parties of Bournemouth for the military-pickle suppers of Farnham.

My aged hostess was a general's widow. The house was filled with old brown photographs showing royalty inspecting guards of honour, a sour-faced Lord Roberts, a girlish face signed in a flourish by a young Queen Mary, and upstairs and downstairs and not only in my lady's but in every chamber, scores of photographs of be-medalled heroes with handlebar moustaches. And on the screen in my bedroom various vice-reines were pasted to watch with obvious disapproval as the ex-street urchin discarded the respectable pyjamas which nothing would induce him to wear throughout a whole night.

Roman Holiday

It was flattering to be the centre of a lot of social entertainment. Historic country houses hidden among woods or standing gracefully in summer meadows awaited my visits. Also, I went occasionally to London and discovered its West End theatres. But although these were idyllic days, a seventeen-year-old soon tires of playing clock-golf with admirals, no matter how famous they may be, or being an audience for senile colonels' reminiscences of India.

The tedium of Farnham was relieved a little by the presence of two spotty Etonians of my own age. They called at Mrs. More-Molyneux's to collect me for the day and tried to instil the niceties of tennis into me. The lack of success became so conspicuous that they dropped tennis in favour of mah-jong, at which I did slightly better. The boys personified charm and consideration. They read poetry and pornography, with the luscious accent native to upper-income-bracket Surrey, later cultivated at the College of the Blessed Mary, and discussed a thousand and one different topics from sex to science and back to sex again. But I thought of them as still being children. What did they know of Bute Street's passions? What, for that matter, did they know of the *real* me, the boy who never knew for years whether he would end up in an Approved School, a school approved of in a rather different sense from the approval given to the school on the Thames?

As much as possible I tried to hide these subversive thoughts from my two companions as the mah-jong tiles clicked on the table. The seasons and flowers, the dragons and winds passed through my fingers until I thought I should die from boredom and gentility. While my neighbour as the East Prevailing Wind would be overcome with joy at getting the limited hand of 'Catch the moon from the bottom of the sea', I would be far away in my own dreams, quite unconscious that I could let off a cannon with my last wind.

A letter came for me from the Catholic priest of Crickhowell in Brecknockshire. He wanted me to visit him. There was much for me to put right with this man. During the previous summer, while missionizing from the churchyard caravan, I had strewn the priest's church with Gospel tracts. On a few occasions I had importuned nuns from the nearby convent and asked then if they were 'born again' Christians. To refuse Father Osborne's invitation would have been a little harsh.

Father Osborne met me off the bus at Abergavenny and took me to his presbytery along the river Usk. By those river banks I had led the singing of Gospel choruses and listened to evil rumours about the convent up the road. Now I was walking through Crickhowell's main street with the parish priest. A Baptist elder at whose house I had stayed on a preaching engagement, came from a garage to spit out some hateful remark. News of my coming as a Roman Catholic fellow-traveller spread through all the valleys where I had once preached. Once again, a throng of 'praying partners' got busy.

Meanwhile I relaxed in the simple and easy atmosphere of the presbytery. Father Osborne sat up late with me at night going over and over many things to which an Ulsterman does not take readily—papal infallibility, transubstantiation, the Immaculate Conception, purgatory. Most important of all, my wavering belief in a God of any sort was expertly dealt with. The nuns whom I had so often rudely accosted in the street now prepared me all sorts of delicacies and I decided to winter in Crickhowell, 'wintering' being a phrase I picked up in Farnham.

But contrary forces were in action. Praying partners were still upholding me at the Throne of Grace. Within a month I was back on their side. This came to pass naturally enough when I went down to the Bible Academy to get my winter clothes. Sister Edna had arrived in her car. She was collecting it at the end of its summer's lease to evangelical activities in Wales, including a Gospel caravan now placed prominently in an orchard in Crickhowell. I could never bear to hurt or distress Sister Edna. When she suggested that I should go with her to Devon to think things over regarding the Roman Church, I accepted readily for I had made no commitments at Farnham or Crickhowell.

While I was in Devon the storm at the Academy broke. The

two warring factions flew at each other's throats and the whole place was closed down temporarily. When matters were finally sorted out, the Academy re-opened. But some of its best students had left in disgust, as well as the Vice-Principal. Brother Edward was among them. He was my last intimate friend in the place.

The Principal wrote to me and asked me to return, for, as usual, he was anxious to keep the number of students up. I felt confused and torn by a hundred conflicting aims. But curiosity got the better of me. I could not resist the temptation to see a new Academy rising from the ashes of the old. Besides, Sister Edna wanted me to go back and finish the course set before me, of becoming a missionary.

So I went back, grateful at least that the storm had burst, in my absence, over heads other than my own. Why, I wondered going down in the train, did I go on pretending? And why did the Academy people keep on fooling themselves and others? The vicious bitterness which both caused and resulted from the Academy's schism masqueraded under their repetitive, monotonous slogan 'We are all one in the Lord'.

CHAPTER VI

Tinkerbell's Miracle

❧❦❧

Any lingering doubts that it was the Lord and not Tinker-bell who was leading me to the peaks of success, now vanished. I had the evidence parcelled up, literally, inside the little brown suitcase which our Bible house colporteur hawked around.

Living 'by faith' was not such a vague business as the uninitiated might suppose. The Lord always provided. We made sure He did. At public meetings we would pray aloud, very loud, for any special needs. As soon as our prayer was over, our eyes could be opened to look swiftly over the bowed heads. We had to be sure that one of the dozen or so regulars was feeling for a fountain pen to sign a cheque. The actual amount required might have been specifically named in the prayer. Our skill in 'living by faith' even went to the extent that we knew where to pray for particular things. It was like shopping.

The Academy's colporteurs called with the case of books at the houses of the local wealthy. And there was one of these big houses which never failed, whether in providing a fat cheque to pay for domestic help at the Bible Academy, or whether in sending a missionary student post-haste to India. Like all the students before me who had helped in hawking the Academy's books, I too found myself passing through the gate of Meron House.

In a few weeks it would be Christmas, a splendid time for reminding the general public that a merry Christmas was a sure-fire way of getting into hell. I was doing a roaring trade in

high-priced books on missionary travel and adventure, and in
de luxe Bibles which replaced the usual merchandise and Gospel
tracts at two shillings per hundred. And from within the depths
of Meron House, Mrs. Curry-Gowan emerged. She had so
many nieces' birthdays to think about, quite apart from her
own daughters' and the female wardens' in the girls' hostel
down the road, to say nothing about Christmas coming.

And had it not been for Tinkerbell my fate at Meron House
would have been no different from scores of other students
who had called there. In common with my predecessors I received the lightest possible handshake from Mrs. Curry-
Gowan's arthritis-gnarled fingers and a glass of ginger-pop.
This, and no more than this, was as far as any of my fellows
had ever got with the old lady. But when I called at the house
with Tinkerbell and the cart to collect an empty trunk, Tinkerbell herself won me favour in Mrs. Curry-Gowan's eyes.

I had swallowed my ginger-pop and was outside climbing
on to the cart ready to drive away when I heard the frail
fingers tapping on the window. Mrs. Curry-Gowan was
beckoning. She called me into the drawing-room and closed
the door behind us. Something obviously troubled her. Her
lined face carried the expression of a person about to unleash
feelings too-long pent up. For one impossible wild moment,
I thought she was about to tell me that she had fallen in love
with me. But no, Mrs. Curry-Gowan took my arm and led me
to the window.

She pointed to Tinkerbell who had deposited a neat heap of
dung on the road. Mrs. Curry-Gowan directed her gaze towards the golden pile and then transferred it to her rose-beds.
Being a lady, Mrs. Curry-Gowan could not bring herself to
say the word 'manure', but in a confidential whisper she asked
me if I would convey it to the rose-beds. Besides Miss Fairweather, there was nobody else in the house, Mrs. Curry-
Gowan explained. And since Miss Fairweather was a lady-
housekeeper, despite the fact that she answered the doorbell,
she could not reasonably be asked to shovel up the golden
balls. I perfectly understood. The rose-beds looked so under-

nourished. Clearly, the mess outside was one answer to a gardener's prayer, and I was another.

And so I became Robert to Meron House, and not just simply the 'Irish student'. Tinkerbell continued to produce the healthful dung for the rose-beds. Every week I collected a case-load from the waste land by the Navvy Mission where Tinkerbell passed her tethered days. Without even a decent interval elapsing, I was invited to luncheon which was considered a great honour at the Academy. Even favourite missionaries home on furlough never got further than drawing-room tea at Meron House. Sister Winifred who fancied her importance as the wife of one of the greatest Bible teachers, had never got beyond the ginger-pop or peppermint cream stage.

One day, Mrs. Curry-Gowan asked me to go to the house early in the morning. I was the only person in the world, she said, whom she could trust with the most important of missions. Indeed, I must be careful that neither her son nor daughters heard of the matter until the manœuvre was complete. Her unmarried sister, Aunt Mabel, was in great danger. And, more to the point, Aunt Mabel's fortune was in danger too.

Aunt Mabel also had a housekeeper. This was Mrs. Lambey. But unlike her opposite number in Meron House, Mrs. Lambey was a working-housekeeper, not a lady. In addition Mrs. Lambey was not 'saved'. On occasions she had been surprised whilst dusting Aunt Mabel's drawing-room with a feather duster in one hand and a lighted cigarette in the other. Unfortunately, Mrs. Lambey was something of a fixture. Uncle Willie, the sisters' brother, had taken Mrs. Lambey into employment many years earlier and she had remained, a thorn in all Christian flesh, ever since.

Nobody, not a single soul, least of all Aunt Mabel, was prepared for what the reading of Uncle Willie's will revealed when he died. He left Mrs. Lambey two thousand pounds and various mortgaged property. Perhaps more than the money, it was the irony which stung Aunt Mabel and Mrs. Curry-Gowan—two thousand pounds for *that* woman who was not even a lady-housekeeper!

Mrs. Curry-Gowan had smarted for years under the living insult of Mrs. Lambey's presence in the family. She had tried with no avail to persuade Aunt Mabel to get rid of Mrs. Lambey. There was a battle by telephone about it every morning. Miss Fairweather had to call the operator as it was quite impossible for Mrs. Curry-Gowan to talk with the unsaved working-housekeeper. When the telephone rang in Aunt Mabel's house it would be answered by, 'This is Mrs. Lambey', to which our lady-housekeeper on our end of the line would reply, 'This is Fairweather'.

With Uncle Willie's death, however, and the outrageous legacy, a climax had been reached. A bundle of Uncle Willie's letters from Lloyd George and Neville Chamberlain was missing. Also unaccounted for was a silver teapot presented to Uncle Willie when he was Lord Mayor.

Mrs. Curry-Gowan had a plan to save the family fortune from further depredation. She spurned her own husband's family fortunes because they came from the heyday of Cardiff's Tiger Bay when their ships were the biggest and most modern to sail out of the Bristol Channel. But her own family were old Cornish bankers, solid as a rock, a family which had never married below or above itself. This stock had produced generations of worthies who were content to be no more and no less than Assay Masters of Tin to the Prince of Wales or Auditors of the Imprest. Not for them were the cheap-jack honours of Cardiff—'The City of Dreadful Knights'.

So, weighty with the knowledge of our visit's importance, I sat beside Mrs. Curry-Gowan as we drove off to restore the family honour and, we hoped, the remains of the family fortune also. *Operation Aunt Mabel* had to be planned to take place on Mrs. Lambey's 'day out'. The working-housekeeper certainly would never allow Aunt Mabel to be taken out of the house and driven off to Meron House to live with her sister, while Mrs. Lambey herself was dismissed. She was as sly as the Serpent in the Garden and any suspicion as to the purpose of our visit would have ruined the whole project.

The journey took forty minutes, but it seemed no time at all because Mrs. Curry-Gowan closed the glass partition separating us from the chauffeur so that he could not eavesdrop on the prayers we offered among the rugs and cushions at the back. Although he had more sense than to show it, the driver was no doubt eaten up with curiosity, for the journey was made normally only on Monday, which was chiropody day.

Mrs. Curry-Gowan wrought herself into a trance of outraged self-righteousness and was commanding the demons in Mrs. Lambey to depart. Demon-possession featured as an important topic at Meron House, never far from either conversation or prayers. At its feet was laid the responsibility for any evil behaviour by any of Mrs. Curry-Gowan's acquaintances.

Arrived at Aunt Mabel's house and duly unloaded, Mrs. Curry-Gowan instructed the driver to wait. Our business, she told him, would be speedy. I stood guard by the drawing-room door lest the wily Mrs. Lambey should surprise us by an unexpected return. Inside, the eighty-four-year-old Mrs. Curry-Gowan urged her even older sister to come away in our car and escape from the Lambey's clutches. Only snatches of the conference came through clearly, but I could guess from Mrs. Curry-Gowan's tone the main drift. I could also tell that she was making no headway for a sternness crept into her voice which always came when her will was being frustrated. After an hour Mrs. Curry-Gowan gave up trying. Aunt Mabel refused to budge from her warm house. Nor would she hear of Mrs. Lambey's dismissal, for the working-housekeeper gave wonderful service and her cooking was irreproachable. Mrs. Curry-Gowan did not help her case by saying that, of course, good cooking was the least one could expect from an ex-barmaid. This cruel jibe never failed to rouse Aunt Mabel, who stoutly maintained that her domestic treasure had never worked in a public house. And indeed, our only concrete evidence against Mrs. Lambey was her cigarette smoking and the housemaid's teacups, that trail of tea-leaves left high and dry on the cup's side which spoke volumes about upbringing and background.

When we got outside again, the driver's face still retained its impassiveness. Without a word we got in. Mrs. Curry-Gowan was silent but I could see from the grim lines about her mouth that she was far from beaten. I felt sorry for God. He would be kept occupied by many more hours of prayer on the subject of Aunt Mabel and Mrs. Lambey.

However, to be behind-the-scenes of these family scandals was a feather in my cap. Not even Mrs. Curry-Gowan's lawyers enjoyed her confidence to such a degree, though they were forever being summoned to Meron House to alter the old lady's will when some relative had newly fallen into disfavour. That I had conquered Meron House, picking, as it were, the choicest plum among the local big houses, earned me the jealousy of many at the Bible Academy.

When I began to spend whole days with the wealthy Curry-Gowan family the jealousy came into the open. Sister Winifred telephoned while I was at Meron House one day and demanded my instant return to the Bible Academy. This made me angry, for I guessed that the excuse would probably be no more than something connected with the Bible depot's shop window or a similar trifling matter. The more Sister Winifred nagged on the telephone the angrier I grew. In the end she threatened me, and I shouted. Calling her by a suitable name I slammed the receiver down.

That, I knew, was the end of my career in the Academy. Only the formality of being thrown out remained now. I determined that this should be as spectacular as possible. At exactly five minutes past ten that night I thundered on the Academy's great double doors, demanding admittance. Five past ten! This sin alone brought me immediately into the presence of the Principal who was already night-shirted and in bed. First, he laid the awful charge against me of returning after ten o'clock curfew. Then, with a look of doom, he asked if I realized that while shouting on the telephone from Meron House at his wife, I had called her 'an old witch'.

He was right about ten o'clock but wrong about the old witch. What I had said was something stronger. But this typically evangelical euphemism annoyed me. Twenty minutes later my bags were packed and a car was on the way down from Meron House to pick me up. I did not look back at the Academy as I sat in the car. Before I got to Mrs. Curry-Gowan's house fresh bed-linen and valances had replaced the dust-sheets in the best guest-room.

Next day when Miss Fairweather cleared the line of Mrs. Lambey, the two sisters got down to their usual morning conference. They had much to say. Robert had come in the middle of the night after the storm and do you know what he called Sister Winifred. Aunt Mabel did not know. 'Well,' and here Mrs. Curry-Gowan crouched over the old-fashioned telephone and drew her tippet shawl closer so that the Austrian housemaid should not hear, 'look in the dictionary, Mabel, and you will see it as the female of dog.'

This great disclosure made, the ear-piece was hung on its hook. It summed Sister Winifred up neatly I thought, that she should have twisted the truth of the matter by saying that I called her an old witch instead of an old bitch. But Mrs. Curry-Gowan understood, though even she could not bring herself to say such a dreadful word.

None of us realized that my flight from the Bible Academy meant that I would be associated for the next four years as the son of the house, living on and off with Mrs. Curry-Gowan. The heavy Victorian gloom of Meron House exactly suited the life between its walls. Yet a kindness dwelt there which had been totally lacking at the Academy. In spite of Mrs. Curry-Gowan's strict adherence to a narrow, religious way of life, I liked her and found no difficulty in calling her 'Mama'.

The ponderous ritual of living in that house exerted a strange hypnosis over me. But Mrs. Curry-Gowan considered herself as being far from old-fashioned. Had she and her husband not been the first in the town with the telephone? Had their's not been the town's first motor car? Indeed, Mrs. Curry-Gowan had longer survived this period itself for she still spoke of 'motoring-clothes and veils'. Even her youngest daughter, a doctor, still had to wear woollen combinations as though man's wit had devised nothing further following their invention. Yet curiously, changes in the world at large were not ignored by Mama. The house on one side had been turned into flats where washing was flown like flags, and on a Sunday too. The house on the other side had become an hotel where people with unashamed Lancashire accents could be heard across our jasmine hedge.

Nevertheless, we were a little world on our own, a microcosm of vanished Victorian manners. We changed into houseshoes on coming in from the garden, though true, Mrs. Curry-Gowan did not altogether approve of the Austrian housemaid leaving the washing in order to rush over and kiss her mistress's arthritic hands at every appearance.

The good Frau lived in one of the next-door flats with her daughter and bootmaker son-in-law. She did not come into Meron House until after breakfast, though in time for family prayers. Since we had no resident housemaid, the preparation of breakfast fell on Miss Fairweather. We all liked the old Frau and the daughter who eventually succeeded her. The son-in-law, however, was a different matter. He drank heavily. One evening when I was out he called at Meron House with shoes he had mended for Mrs. Curry-Gowan. The man came to the door and knocked. And here Miss Fairweather displayed her unsuspected depths of courage for while everybody else hid, she went alone and unarmed to the door and opened it, defenceless, to face the wine-bibber and take the shoes in.

Some time passed before I became accustomed to Miss Fairweather. She was a small, dainty creature, who climbed the staircase with asthmatic difficulty to suck a secret supply of oranges in her room. Naturally, Miss Fairweather was 'saved' and she broke bread with the Plymouth Brethren. But lady and Christian though she undoubtedly was, Mrs. Curry-Gowan never trusted her with the housekeeping keys for longer than the exercise of her duties demanded.

After hearing the morning postman come through the garden, I would lie on in bed waiting for Miss Fairweather to wake and go along the corridor. She went to collect the linen bag of keys from Mama's bedside table. Even then I could not get up, for Miss Fairbrother was so slow and took aeons to empty her C.A.—Certain Article.

In some of its appointments, Meron House seemed to hark back to a pre-Victorian period. Although the upper floors were adequately equipped with what are known as modern conveniences, each bedroom nevertheless had to have its C.A. enshrined in a ponderous throne-like commode. When I first went to live there my health was not good. Mama put me under medical supervision straight away when she learnt that I had spent the first twelve years of my life dodging in and out of hospital and tuberculosis clinics. She had no doubts that the best thing for a young fellow like me was to be 'regular'. But keeping regular was a most frightful business. The slightest hint of constipation and I would be subjected to a most detailed catechism, until I felt like the boy in the 'When did you last see your father' picture. Should I appear downstairs in the morning and be pronounced 'off colour' then I would be told to go upstairs again after family prayers. There, all ready, my personal enema would be waiting for me together with quantities of hot soapy or salty water. And I had to pump myself and contain myself for a specified time. It was a nightmare to me and I saw quickly that the only way out was to feign treatment and merely to stay in my room.

When Miss Fairweather got the bag of keys she unlocked the bathroom and filled Mama's brass can with hot water. Being now a member of the family, its youngest, I was allowed into Mama's room before the bed was made. I greeted her on both cheeks and received in return a special kiss on the forehead. This indeed was a mark of favour for it distinguished me from the other cheek-pecking which went on during the day among the comings and goings of relatives and friends.

And of all the rooms in Meron House, that house which finally changed and set its stamp upon the Belfast street urchin who, not so many years before, had put sorrel leaves between stale potato farls, of all its rooms Mama's bedroom was the heart. It could have served admirably as a museum of Victoriana, though, in fact all of its various bits and pieces of impedimenta were used as they had been for decades. Dominating the time-proof, worm-proof, immoveable furniture, the medicine chests and the bric-á-brac flotsam of foreign travel, was the vast bed of brass replete with hangings and winged brackets, and an ottoman. Outside the window was a balcony to which a large telescope had been fixed in the days when the Curry-Gowans used it to watch their own ships' movements in and out of the Bristol Channel.

Downstairs, the dining-room carried on where Mama's room left off for it was literally a museum. Here, in glass-fronted cases lining the walls stood evidence of the Curry-Gowan wealth and the history of its accumulation. The shelves bore hundreds of specimens taken from typical cargoes carried by the family ships—miniature bales of cotton and bags of coffee, tiny loads of Parana pine and dozen upon dozen of grubby-looking mineral specimens. The dining-room sideboard carried models of a dolomite mine and pithead shafts from former Curry-Gowan mines.

Nor was expression of the family achievement confined to the dining-room. Landing and staircase walls were hidden by heavily-framed paintings of the family ships, nicely spaced between Mad John Martin's melodramatic *Destruction of Herculaneum* and *The Great Day of His Wrath*. Here also, incongruous and unlikely, hung the Rope. This was in case of fire. Was it conceivable if flames should ever destroy Meron House that the slow, crippled Mama and Miss Fairweather would actually toss the Rope overboard to dangle between the flights of stairs, and then climb down like sailors? No, it was not conceivable. But they believed it was and I did not care to disillusion them.

Brass water-can delivered, Miss Fairweather's next task was to help Mama into her elastic stockings and when, following all, the last comb had been set in place around Mama's cottage-loaf hair, both ladies started the great journey downstairs, having made certain the bed-clothes were flung right back and the windows opened wide to save them from the horror of hot-beds.

Breakfast and family prayers followed and then Miss Fairweather donned a bib-apron, put her spectacles on, and began to prepare the vegetables for luncheon. At eleven o'clock she crept upstairs again for a secret orange. During this interval Mama would ask me to go into the kitchen with her. We made a bee-line for the refuse bucket were might be seen signs of Miss Fairweather's inefficiency. More often than not it was plain that the lady-housekeeper had sinned once more. She peeled such thick skins from the potatoes that Mama, crippled though her fingers were, could take the skins from the bucket and peel slithers of potato from them.

Waste was a sin. This struck me as the most odd of all the eccentricities in Meron House. Every day a lot of bread was wasted, because all sides and crusts of bread were cut off and thrown away. From my country experience, I knew how this bread could be used. In the first week I collected three bucketfuls and gave them to the people in one of the flats next door who kept chickens in the garden. The ladies of Meron House frowned on this, but when our neighbours began to give us presents of fresh eggs, they thought it a master-stroke of mine.

Obviously, I did not fall into the waster class like Miss Fairweather. Mama made her suffer for a carelessly abandoned lettuce leaf or an ounce of parsnip. Nevertheless such parsimony was related mostly to minor domestic matters. If a missionary came to tea with tales of need in desert or jungle he would seldom leave the house without a fat cheque.

Rhythms and patterns of daily routine began almost at once when I had settled permanently into Meron House. Although, unlike Farnham, there was no social life to occupy me, my days nevertheless were full and interesting enough to make me forget that the Bible Academy had ever existed or that training for a missionary within its sad walls had been the occasion of my leaving Ireland and the old life. I was certainly getting on well, for in making herself my new Mama, Mrs. Curry-Gowan was set on making a Christian gentleman out of me. The prospect of this did not altogether displease me.

I was expected to spend my mornings in study to make up

the deficiencies in my education as a boy. And to add the graces to the virtues Mama also had a music teacher for me, a woman whose patience was monumental when brought face to face with my unmusicalness. I liked music, or at least certain kinds of music. But to struggle with the printed note and the bewildering complexity of the keyboard were things quite beyond me. Nevertheless, Mama insisted for she was herself imbued with music and before arthritis took its toll of her hands, she played the piano well. Though she winced when I pounded the keyboard, changing tonality into atonality and advancing some innocent eighteenth-century piece by a century and a half so that it emerged complete with the Viennese twelve notes and discords, Mama stuck to her guns. Apart from the actual tuition I had to practise for at least an hour every day, usually with Mama in attendance as audience. My mistakes and clumsiness wounded her. But she probably suffered no more from this than she did, for instance, from visitors who sat in the drawing-room with their feet turned in.

There was also French, considered indispensable, not so much as a language but as a social accomplishment. Mama instructed me in French herself. But I fear that much of what she taught fell like seed in the parable on to stony ground. It was not the difficulties of grammar, or even the pronunciation which confounded me so much as the France with which I was confronted. It was the France of the 1870s and Mama's girl-hood where she spent three years being 'finished'. There was precious little to attract a seventeen-year-old Irish boy about a young lady's Paris, and I did not then know I would be a frequenter of Paris myself.

Mama almost regarded her French 'finishing' as of equal importance with being 'saved'. She was certain, for instance, that Aunt Mabel behaved in such a 'queer' way because she had been sent to a German finishing-school. Questions of taste and of value were involved here. True it was that Aunt Mabel came back from Germany able to do excellent poker work, and able even to finish *The Times* crossword puzzle before breakfast. But where was the point of such accomplishments when the woman made a fool of herself over things like Mrs. Lambey and Lloyd George's letters? Mama was even reduced to telephoning her sister at night as well as in the morning. Much to Mama's amazement and horror, Aunt Mabel listened to 'ITMA'. To catch her in the wicked act, and persuade her to switch the programme off, was, in Mama's view, the least she could do to help preserve Aunt Mabel's soul.

CHAPTER VII

Kind Hearts and Baronets

❧❦❧

At about noon of each working day, I was allowed to lay the books of Latin and mathematics aside and to help Mama into her outdoor shoes. If the weather was very fine we would take a walk to Rendezvous Corner. This was her name for a shady and sheltered corner of the park near the sea-front promenade. Mama could scarcely have made the journey alone because she was afraid of the town's dogs which always seemed to rendezvous at the corner. Though shocked at bodily functions, like most evangelicals, Mama's objection to the dogs was not so much their orgiastic antics as the fact that in their exultant rushes they were liable to knock her down, for her legs were far from sturdy.

Once arrived at Rendezvous Corner we would sit, Mama recovering from the effort of walking a whole furlong from the house. Breath regained she would begin to talk and to talk with a freedom not possible within Meron House's four walls because these sometimes had ears. Mama would give me her twisted little hands to keep warm in my own as she unburdened herself.

Mama's life was hedged about by so many difficulties and worries. Even the wooden garden seat on which we sat at Rendezvous Corner had its unpleasant associations, for it was on that seat where Uncle Willie had got rid of yet more of the family fortune. A little girl had been sitting on the seat one day, and because she talked to him the old man had gone home and added a codicil to his will, leaving the previously unknown child a legacy, which naturally diminished the leavings for Mama's own children. 'Willie was queer,' Mama would sigh for the hundredth time, 'giving all that money to a strange child.'

And so the conversation moved from the inexhaustibly fascinating contemplation of Uncle Willie to his and Mama's Cornish childhood. From what I could gather this childhood itself had been subject to strange events. Mama talked of people who had been buried alive not in some pagan ritual but simply by mistake. She confidently hoped that Christ's Second Coming would occur during her lifetime. In the same practical tone with which she would order the car for a visit to Aunt Mabel, Mama would point out how much better it would be to meet the Lord in the air (presumably borne by some giant kind of swan wings) than to risk the chance of being buried when not quite dead, perhaps to wake up in the coffin and gnaw one's own arms which sometimes happened, as she had been told, in France.

She told the story of a grave-thief in Bodmin who opened a vault to steal rings and jewellery but was frightened away by the coffin's occupant who showed distinct signs of life. Perhaps, mused Mama on more than one day, that was why Willie had left their ninety-six-years-old mother shrouded so long in the drawing-room until decency and hygiene demanded her burial. Uncle Willie had made provision that at his own death his jugular vein should be cut, just to make sure, though when cremation became acceptable he waived this.

Mama would tell me yet again about a particularly fat cousin who had actually burst in her coffin. And then, inevitably, if the talk were of this kind we would return to the all-absorbing subject of trying to compose Mama's own epitaph. Our talks in the park, however, were not all always so morbid. Sometimes I would hear all about the great fortitude shown by some member of the family, perhaps Aunt Gale who, poor soul, was struck down and had to manage with no more than a hundred pounds pin-money.

A permanent regret of mine was that I never met Uncle

Willie. He died two years before I went to Meron House. Nevertheless, I felt his presence and knew I had reason to bless him, because of his friendship with the Misses Curry. In sixty years he had failed to screw up enough courage to ask Miss Frederica's hand in marriage. That branch of the Curry family was even wealthier than Mama's own and I was allowed to travel to London from time to time to see Frederica and Beatrice and to collect my birthday and Christmas present cheques. Their brother, Sir Clifford Curry, was Mama's own great friend. Though she never said so, I think she was sorry that she had not married him. In every day's prayers she blessed Sir Clifford on account of his legacy to her girls' hostel which enabled them to purchase a nice big property.

Mama's two brothers-in-law were Sir Clifford's rivals in business but she despised them although they were equally famous as philanthropists. But Mama's fingers would press mine in agitation as she spoke of the brothers-in-law whom she denounced more for their vulgarity of spirit than for material crimes. What hard work it had been for Mama, trying to persuade them to wait for baronetcies instead of straining after the first available common knighthood. She had similarly dissuaded her sister-in-law from calling their new brick house a 'hall', although today this mansion of more than a hundred rooms has collected a railway station and a town round itself.

Nevertheless, the brothers-in-law were gentlemen for they too came from Cornwall. In Mama's mind she distrusted the Welsh but strangely, thought highly of the Irish. In the good old days no household had been complete without an Irish maid, usually a lady's maid who could wear her mistress's pearls while asleep, so bringing out a lustre which only an Irish skin could.

Mama believed firmly in the superiority of the Cornish over the Welsh. Although Sir Clifford Curry was known as a Welsh colliery owner, he had gone to dear Cornwall to get his parliamentary seat. Contrariwise the Cornish brothers-in-law had represented Welsh constituencies. A great difference was that Clifford was a Liberal politician whereas the brothers-in-law sat with the Tories. Mama could not bear to think about the Liberal decline of power. She hated to put her election cross against the Conservative candidate's name. But she had no alternative, for Socialism was her natural enemy. Mama never recovered from the blow which the nationalization of the railways gave her, for she had large sums invested in them.

Mention of the Liberals also upset Mama because she could not hear even the world 'Liberal' without being reminded of Lloyd George's letters and Aunt Mabel's working-housekeeper. Her dislike of Socialism was no matter of abstract ideals but of mundane affairs. She feared strikes most of all, and avoided reading newspapers in case there should be reports or rumours of strikes. They were of the Devil. If all employers had been as good as Sir Clifford there would have been no Socialism and no strikes. He had been a Christian and saw to it that the 'handmaid and manservant within the gate' were properly attended to.

Strikes struck at Mama's concern for her own fortune which she had no desire to lose. Strikes during the 1920s had brought about the ruin of the coal-exporting side of the family fleet. The grasping, cheap-jack knights had asked for it, of course, Mama would allow in more relaxed moments. But in the general débâcle, the innocent had suffered with the guilty. And now, with the government nationalizing mines as well as railways, it really was time the Lord appeared in His Second Coming and stopped the rot.

Rendezvous Corner became a ritual, a pleasure denied only by wind or rain. And always Mama drifted back to the bygone days in Cornwall. I can still see the special messenger driving from London to tell Mama's father of attempts on Queen Victoria's life. I can hear the indignant father meeting Mama on her return from being 'finished' in France, and almost pulling her ears off because she was wearing ear-rings. And so often did Mama talk about Launceston that I can never now dissociate that town from 'the Oscar Wilde trouble'.

Mama would never have used a word like 'homosexuality' but she certainly talked often and at length about 'the Oscar

Wilde trouble', because it had all started for her in their Cornish home. As a girl she had watched the Reverend Thomas Walters coming up the drive to tutor her brother Willie at Latin. And Mama would ask her own mother if she could send an old pinafore to poor Minnie, the Vicar's daughter. That this same Minnie Walters became the Marchionness of Queensberry never ceased to amaze Mama. But the world of Mama and the old Cornish gentry was shaken further when Minnie died and the Marquis married a fishmonger's daughter from Cardiff.

But at least Minnie had provided a link with the terrible *demi-monde* of her brother-in-law Lord Alfred Douglas. For Mama perhaps nothing in her lifetime had disturbed her notion of propriety so much as Oscar and his friend. We seldom left Rendezvous Corner without a reference to 'the trouble'.

On the way back, we often walked beyond our own house and garden and went for a little way past the neighbours. Mama did not see the American children playing baseball in the garden, or the rows of unwashed milk-bottles from the flats. They did not exist for her. In their place were the private houses and their gardens as they had been sixty years before. She peopled them with those who had seen her arrival as a young girl from Cornwall.

There had been Lord Plymouth who prospered even more than the brothers-in-law, yet his daughter had married a cricketer. How queer the world was, really. And in the next house, the Russells had lived and although they were carriage-folk, they had never been gentlefolk. Mrs. Russell practised on the piano for five hours a day, yet it was an embarrassment when one invited her to eat for the same clever fingers 'painted with her knife' at table.

And beyond Mrs. Russell's, as Mama approached the last house, sadness would shade her voice. Because of the war, the house swarmed with vulgar, screaming girls. The Admiralty had turned the place into a Wrens' land-ship. And for Mama, this was a much worse thing to see than even the mating cockerels in Mrs. Russell's former shrubbery. Not even when the King and Queen had visited the Wrens, was the conversion redeemed.

This showed the extent of Mama's disapproval, for she held royalty in deep respect. She had recently seen a fortune-teller's sign announcing Queen Mary's patronage. By nightfall, Mama had a letter in the post to Marlborough House, reminding the dowager queen of her happy girlhood session of evangelical praise with good Princess Mary of Teck. Mama's favourite member of the royal family, however, was Princess Helena Victoria. While on a visit to South Wales this lady had distinguished herself by buying Uncle Willie some cough drops for his throat.

Though Mama's talk was as frank as her evangelical scruples would allow, she seldom spoke evil against any of her multitudinous relatives and neighbours. But when we wandered slowly back to the house for luncheon, she would often be attacked by remorse for having dragged so many in-laws or cousins and their faults into her talking. Scores of times I later found the old lady on her bedroom balcony doing her spiritual exercises. 'Give me a prick, Lord, give me a prick!' She would call skywards, meaning that God was to pin-prick her pride.

Mama had always been acutely aware of the dangers in hypocrisy. With every endeavour she had tried to practise what she preached. When she came to Wales as the young bride and had been offered Lord Romilly's house, she refused it and took modest Meron House instead. And in the summer, when the girls' hostel was full, she would offer free accommodation to north country mill-girls.

Before the luncheon gong sounded Mama had to go upstairs to unlock one of the drawers in the massive wardrobe in order to take from it another bunch of keys which included the key to the drawing-room cupboard where the boiled sweets were kept. Sweets, like most things, were still rationed, but there were always several tins to carry into the dining-room. On special days there would be halva from Egypt too. Usually, however, our meal ended with a humbug and a peppermint cream which sat throughout the other courses on a side plate like a couple of specimens from the mineral showcases round the walls.

We sat solemnly chewing and sucking until after the concluding grace, when Mama and I made a procession back to the drawing-room with the tins of sweets. Half an hour afterwards Miss Fairweather knocked on the door and came in to surrender the housekeeping keys before going to her room to sleep. Whether she wished it or not, the lady-housekeeper had to make herself scarce until sharp at a quarter to five, for that was when Miss Violet left the kitchen.

Violet was Mama's elder daughter. And although Violet had received her education at the best of public schools she had always been 'queer'. Unfortunately, hers was not Uncle Willie's queerness of eccentricity, but a decided, though comparatively mild, madness. Mama blamed her husband for Violet's condition because he had forced their daughter to lie prone on the floor for hours on end every day without moving, in a vain attempt to correct her stooping back and rounded shoulders. His achievement was a huge and fat woman of over sixty and a joke in the town.

Not until four o'clock in the afternoon did Violet get up, to eat a meal. If she was not out of the kitchen by a quarter to five when Miss Fairweather went to collect her keys again, there was always a row. This, like all the major domestic crises, ended with Mama standing at the foot of the stairs and addressing Violet's possessing demons—'In the precious name of the Lord Jesus I command you to leave this dear child.'

Violet's next two hours were passed in the bathroom, the door of which remained wide open. Violet was unaware of anyone else's existence while following her favourite occupation. She filled the washbasin until it almost ran over. Then she stood with her hands resting in it, and gazed with peculiar intensity at her own reflection. At seven o'clock this ungainly Narcissus went out of the house, an extraordinary figure with curly white hair and steel-rimmed glasses embedded in her pudgy childish face. In the town she sat in cheap cafés talking to anybody who would listen about a First War soldier called Randal who had promised to come back and marry her.

When our own supper was over and hot-water bottles and night-comforters had been carried upstairs, the day's last job began—the heating of Violet's water. All rooms and cupboards had to be locked up because of Violet. She was apt to remove things from the house and give them away to the first person she met outside. And since she spent the night roaming about the house it was necessary to have such chattels as there were well out of her reach. When she came in from her pathetic wanderings round the town, Violet expected to find her three large jugs of hot water ready together with a specific number of toast slices.

We could not expect to remain quietly in our rooms if Violet found one of her jugs gone cold so that it could not top up the pot of strong tea also left on the stairs, or if she saw that she was one piece of toast short. The water, the tea and the toast together with other food had to be left on the stairs for Violet herself to carry up to the night-nursery because Miss Fairweather, being a lady-housekeeper, could hardly be expected to do so. In any case, Violet preferred to sit on the stairs with her food until early next day.

Violet had free use of the old night-nursery where a bed was placed. The hallway and stairs were open to her and, of course, one of the lavatories. This was her kingdom through the hours of darkness. Goodness knows what fantasies possessed her until such time as she heard Miss Fairweather's alarm clock defeating night and the demons like the crowing cock of medieval magic. Violet vanished like a wraith when the rest of the household began to stir.

Meron House's day ended at about half-past ten when Miss Fairweather got out the linen bag and put her keys inside. I would be having a last session of prayer with Mama as the tiny woman came round the great brass bed and placed her insignia of office on the bedside table ready for the following day. We bid her good night, and prayed earnestly that she would not cough in the night. If she did, and brought up a speck of blood, we realized that it would be a cold luncheon because Miss Fairweather would be away off to see the specialist with the speck carefully preserved in a handkerchief.

At last I was free to go to bed myself. My room afforded a wonderful view across the Bristol Channel. On many evenings I could see the tiny waves in the moonlight racing across the sandy harbour almost immediately below the house. On clear, still nights, or if the wind was in the right direction, I could hear lovers in the shrubbery of Rendezvous Corner. But in spite of the 'queer' life I was leading in Meron House, I did not feel at all imprisoned in my room with its C.A. and the door locked against the spiritual 'pestilence that walketh in darkness'. By all concerned it was felt that my soul had already taken its share of the similar 'destruction that wasteth at noon-day'.

In any case, I had no wish to leave my room until next morning. It would have been difficult to negotiate the stairs and big Violet surrounded with her hot water jugs and toast.

CHAPTER VIII

A Queer World

꧁꧂

An odd thing about Mama was her taste in music, books and entertainment. As strictly evangelical as anyone at the Bible Academy regarding the blind, unreasoning faith in the 'second birth', she had nevertheless an inquiring mind. So far as the arts were concerned Mama held extremely un-evangelical preferences. She played Grieg on the piano rather than Moody and Sankey. At her bedside were the works of Oliver Wendell Holmes, *The Professor at the Breakfast Table* being the favourite.

Unlike other strict evangelicals Mama did not fear direct contamination from the Devil by listening to the wireless, though she acknowledged him as the Prince of the Air. Mama did not listen indiscriminately, however, and most programmes were regarded as evil, particularly 'ITMA' the most sinful of all. But on the other hand she could hardly wait from one instalment to the next of *Just William*. And *Jane Eyre*, when dramatized by the BBC, was irresistible to Mama. Naturally I could not listen in the drawing-room to the radio in case some praying-partners came in. But it was odd how Mama followed me out to the kitchen when the episodes from that 'worldly' novel were being broadcast.

Mama also loved poetry. She peppered her conversation with verse quotations, notably from *The Jackdaw of Rheims* and *Matilda told such dreadful lies*. For some reason I never fathomed, the Jackdaw fascinated Mama. She would interrupt one of our intimate conversations at Rendezvous Corner—perhaps in the middle of telling me yet again about 'wee Charlie' her still-born eldest child, to recite,

> *And six little singing-boys—dear little souls!*
> *In nice clean faces, and nice white stoles.*

But through what remained of the summer I had grown accustomed to Mama's inconsistencies and eccentricities. Summer persisted well into October and I still swam every day. Mama found no objection in my going to the beach, providing somebody went with me in case of an emergency. More often than not, however, Mama came herself. This was the same sort of gesture as the fire-escape rope hanging over the stairs at Meron House. Mama could not get in or out of her bath without help. I could not see her plunging fully-clothed into the sea to rescue me if I got into difficulties. Fully-clothed it certainly would have been, if at all, because Mama's ideas of decency were few and forceful. It embarrassed me to have her there on the beach, because of the towel I had to change beneath. This vast tent-like, bobble-fringed garment was so designed that not only would observers fail to see my 'private parts' but myself also. Mama also insisted that I wear a rubber bathing cap in the water. She believed that contact with sea water caused baldness. Since my unruly mop of hair was a source of delight to her it would hardly have been kind to cause her the same anxiety about my hair as she was having about her own cottage loaf coils which were sadly greying and thinning.

While on the beach, Mama allowed herself to indulge in a little fantasy. To her I was Oliver Wendell Holmes's tall young oysterman and she was full of pride to see me striking far out into the sea. I think she realized after a time how tired I grew of hearing *The Ballad of the Oysterman*. But she still handed me the tent dressing gown with,

> *I read it in the story-book, that, for to kiss his dear,*
> *Leander swam the Hellespont—and I will swim this here.*

This sequence of events when I went swimming began to cloy the pleasure and I was glad when the end of October brought chill winds and dull skies and I could go to the town's swimming baths where, of course, Mama would not follow. My trips to the baths were often followed by visits to Aunt Mabel's for tea where I spied out the land regarding any further attempts by Mrs. Lambey to steal the family fortune. In this way, I spent whole afternoons and evenings away from Meron House. Cardiff's Bute Street had not changed. Neither had I.

The kind of innocent but necessary hypocrisy that I had adopted at the Bible Academy now stood me in good stead again, allowing satisfaction to the two, but opposed, sides of my nature. I kept up with old acquaintances around the seamen's pools and cafés, where there were always hot bodies heavy with garlic and desire. There were always the red-biddy boys and African drums pounding in the tenement below. There were always work-shy bums 'on the job' with a coarse humour which transformed the leaky gas brackets and the smelly rooms into a kind of fetid paradise.

When I returned to Meron House after an hour or two in Bute Street, however, I was not assailed by the same guilt feelings as I used to be at the Bible Academy. And also, in Mama's house, I gradually discovered that the same need for escape did not exist. Bute Street's bright glitter became tarnished. Eventually I went to Cardiff for the kind of relief and in the kind of way that the suburban man goes to Soho. And in the same way I felt glad when I left for the train back to Meron House again. For with Mama, strangely and incongruously, I had found again the peace and the happiness I lost when I left Fermanagh to work in the grime of Belfast's docklands.

In comparison with the discipline and asceticism of the Bible Academy, life at Meron House was free and easy and Mama did not disapprove of my going to the cinema. She even refrained from calling the cinema 'the seat of the scornful'. And again, in an astonishing way for an evangelical, strict in most other things, Mama thoroughly approved of J. Arthur Rank and his wife who sent her a cheque every year from his cinema profits for the girls' hostel.

Mama loved to tell the story of old Joseph Rank, Lord Rank's miller father, who, years before, had gone to visit Mama and her husband. There had been so much mud on the road that Mama's coachman had to give old Rank a piggy-back into the house. And like themselves the Ranks kept a good Methodist home where The Plan, a quarterly list of local preachers, was held in respect. Although Mama's honeymoon had consisted of a tour round the English cathedrals, she was strictly 'chapel' and took Aunt Mabel's used copies of the *Methodist Recorder* every week.

My own Sundays at Meron House became swamped with engagements from The Plan, though apart from this I no longer accepted preaching engagements. The need for the drug-like stimulus they had given me seemed to have died down through living at Meron House.

Besides tolerating the cinema, Mama also condoned pipe-smoking in moderation, for men only, of course. She acknow-ledged some relations in one of the big tobacco families, in token of which there were actually jars of pipe tobacco standing about the house. Mama did not play too heavily on the theme of this particular family connection. But she did show signs of disappointment when the tobacco firm itself failed to buy some of her sister-in-law's worm-eaten heirlooms. These pieces of furniture were blazoned with the family coat-of-arms, but the magnates were not interested.

Although motion pictures and tobacco were permitted, alcohol definitely was not. Mama had almost refused to marry her husband because her father-in-law would not at first con-sent to a dry wedding. Never for a moment did Mama doubt that the Almighty was up above in a big nightshirt recording every secret sin of Miss Fairweather and every pint of beer drawn at the local pub. 'He watereth the hills from His chambers,' she would say and then sing a temperance hymn on seeing wine-bibbers passing the gate,

A song, a song for water fair,
As pure and free as mountain air!

114

A Queer World

A song, a song for water fair,
As pure and free as mountain air!

Mama's idea of a drunkard was personified in a neighbour called Andrew Mellon. But something had gone wrong with the Lord's justice in this particular instance. Like Mama, Andrew Mellon was one of the remaining few who had not been obliged to carve up their houses into flats. We were given to understand that drink was the downfall of families and family fortunes, and that this was a God-ordained state of things. Andrew Mellon, unfortunately and obstinately did not fit into this pattern. Mama knew that he went twice a day to the Yacht Club where he drank like a fish. Yet in spite of this, the man was growing wealthier and wealthier, prospering as though the Lord were on his side, whereas Mama's own fortunes were getting smaller year by year.

Knowing her prodigal generosity, Mama's husband had made a trust of his capital which she was to enjoy for her lifetime and which thereafter would go to their three children. If these offspring died without issue the money would revert to the husband's nephews. And here was the secret dolour of Mama's life. None of her three children had married and they were now past it. A wilderness stretched before Mama, years in which all that money, instead of going to leper colonies and missions to the Jews, would be squandered by the nephews, one of whom was certainly a wine-bibber for she had seen a newspaper report of his attendance at a cocktail party.

So far as money was concerned all that Mama could do was to spend her income generously and take special needs out of her own personal estate. Demands on her purse were heavy. During my first month at Meron House Mama was obliged to sign over mortgages on some property to a needy missionary.

Little wonder then that Mama prayed aloud during the winter months, after finding from which direction the wind was blowing, 'We are but a feeble folk like the conies in the rocks Lord, and only Thou canst gather the north wind in Thy fists.'

Mama dreaded storms. They frightened her, but worse, in the morning, the builder and his men had to come and crawl over the roof to make sure that no slate was loose. And there another cheque was gone which might have provided blackboards in the new Venezuelan school, or have bought miles of bandages for the dear mission hospital on the Nile.

Yet it was she herself who ordered the builder to come without fail after every storm whether damage had been done or not. It was she who gave the annual order in the summer for the whole house to be repainted, even down to garden sheds and coal bunkers. But to Mama Meron House was a trust of which the Lord saw fit to make her steward. And she was keeping it up, not for her husband's memory, but so that the dear children might bless her in years to come. In maintaining Meron House in ship-shape fashion, Mama knew that Violet would never have to give up playing water-babies in the night-nursery in order to make way for real babies. Before she died, Mama saw her younger daughter paralysed and bed-ridden under the same roof, and Violet shut away in a home.

Meanwhile the 'worldly' nephews bred like rabbits. It was not surprising, therefore, that Mama averted her eyes from *The Times*'s births and christenings columns, those reminders in black and white of her own children's barrenness. When some poor creature from the girls' hostel got herself into trouble it seemed like another sword piercing Mama's heart. How did such girls manage it? And then Aunt Mabel would telephone and announce another grandchild for Mrs. Lambey. Yet not a suitor came in the gate of Meron House, where even poor Violet had her 'bottom drawer' stuffed, though naturally she did not keep the key of it herself.

The occupants of Meron House were the victims of grim irony. Though they possessed, or could have, all that money could buy, the simple joys escaped their grasp. Mama understood that she would never have grandchildren, and she grieved over this as though bereaved. To ease the ache and fill the emptiness, Mama looked to Roberto, as she called me. If nothing more, I brought laughter to the lincrusta and velvet corners of Meron House. Mama's eyes ran with tears at my French pronunciation. Her thinly-fleshed ribs ached with laughing at some of my evacuee stories. She wished not only to possess me in the present but she wanted my past also. Mama loved to hear of my adventures in Fermanagh on various farms and encouraged me to write frequently to Maggie and Christy.

My Belfast life prior to Fermanagh was another matter, however. Mama had once seen a photograph of my mother and had disapproved. I never fully knew why. Perhaps Big 'Ina was too 'common' for Mama, or perhaps my mother's sensuous mouth and clear, alluring eyes were interpreted by the old lady as those of a worldly woman. And also, Mama's favourite missionary society was the Egypt General Mission founded by the seven young men from Belfast. This brought Mama and me mutual acquaintances from Ulster. From one of these people Mama learned of Big 'Ina's lovers and about her occasional jaunts to the pub. This, of course, would never do. Yet, in spite of herself, Mama found as much fascination in Big 'Ina as she did in 'the Oscar Wilde trouble', and for similar reasons. The nature of my parents and of my early upbringing was a subject reserved specially for the secrecy of Rendezvous Corner. Mama would go over the subject again and again, as though to extract the last drop from such a juicy topic.

Because of the old lady's favourite missionary society, started by the seven young men from Belfast, she already had more than usual interest in the city. But this went further. Mama's whole evangelical world of fashion, in its heyday before the turn of the century, centred round a girl from Belfast—Laura Bell. Mama knew Laura Bell after the girl became the great Mrs. Thistlethwayte and a revivalist as renowned as Spurgeon himself. When Mama was young, her greatest joy lay in going up to London and to Mrs. Thistlethwayte's gospel tea-parties in Grosvenor Square, where dear Mr. Gladstone was often of the party.

Like others present on such occasions, Mama knew that the hostess had good reason to sign herself 'A sinner saved by grace through faith in the Lamb of God'. Crowds flocked to see the woman evangelist who, a few years before, had been the centre of scandalized attention by society. Her presence at the opera house, for instance, would bring the whole audience to its feet on her departure, for none wished to miss a glimpse of London's most notorious beauty.

Mr. Gladstone told Mrs. Thistlethwayte that he intended to resign before he told Queen Victoria. But how did the former Laura Bell, the shopgirl from Belfast, get the famous ring from Prince Jung Bahadoor which she returned during the Indian Mutiny, so causing her lover's Gurkha regiments to remain faithful to the British Crown? Laura Bell was not merely 'the greatest beauty of the age' as T. H. Escott, the historian of London clubs, called her. Nor was she only the innocent model of the popular picture called *The Nun*. Laura was, as Sir William Hardman wrote 'the Queen of London whoredom'.

Mama herself had fallen under this amazing creature's spell. And although she greatly admired the leader of evangelical society, it was Mrs. Thistlethwayte's testimony which most thrilled Mama. What rejoicing and thanks there were at this proof of the Lord's strong power and of His infinite forgiveness. And here, Mama would draw comparison between Laura Bell and Big 'Ina. For it was perfectly plain to Mama, that my mother was as big a sinner as the unconverted Laura Bell, an opinion enhanced by the fact that Big 'Ina had been born Georgina Bell—of the selfsame family. But in Mama's view, whereas Laura Bell had given up her evil ways to glow for the Lord, my own mother back in Ireland had done exactly the opposite. She had apparently forsaken her evangelical upbringing and consorted with lovers—and chosen them from among common working men.

Mama's immediate crusade was to save me from such a background. She intended that I should shine like Laura and not lack lustre like Big 'Ina. Yet Mama's intentions produced the opposite to the desired effect. She merely made me see how much I loved my mother. Mama, placed in similar circumstances to Big 'Ina's, would never have had the grit and stamina to walk through winter snow with holes in her shoes at five in the morning to stoke boilers or steal bread so that her children could eat.

I was deeply fond of Mama. But the dry kisses of Meron House meant nothing when I thought of Big 'Ina's last farewell wink at the tram-stop back in Belfast. I derived secret satisfaction when Mama gave me a present of money for I would send it off to Belfast, knowing that Big 'Ina and her boyfriend would have a night out on it. Such things remained secret, however, and I confided to nobody my longings and concern for the life I had left behind me in Ireland. Occasionally Mama would ask if I had heard from *her*, as she referred, perhaps even in jealousy, to Big 'Ina. From this *her* I gauged the extent of Mama's disapproval of Big 'Ina, for Mama called Aunt Mabel's housekeeper *it*.

Not for the first and certainly not for the last time in my life, I was leading two lives. I even took up a London monomark address for my Belfast letters. I could not bear Mama's scrutiny into every crevice of my life. Particularly unbearable were Mama's sneers about Big 'Ina's envelopes which she never addressed herself but got a boy-friend or somebody in the post office to write. Mama liked to keep her eye on all my outgoing mail as well. Many of my letters with the Meron House address were Collins to Mama's friends, and she intended that I should make the right impression.

When I left Ireland I had several hundred pounds, gathered over the years from rabbit trapping and other savings. Until my twelfth year, my life had been so scarred by poverty that I swore never to be poor again. My nest-egg grew into a substantial security. Mama thoroughly approved and encouraged me to write endearing letters, and sometimes verse also, to her wealthy friends. Although the Sermon on the Mount made it plain that the poor were blessed, on the other hand it did not specifically say that the rich were not.

These letters had to have a strong Biblical flavour, and especially the verse so that it could be read aloud by and to these aged and wealthy friends of Mama's. And there I would sit in the drawing-room dressed up to suit the part of poet while all the old dears chuckled my praises between each verse of something like:

> *The Temple gates are shut*
> *And the cool marble washed,*
> *And the old priests are laid*
> *Row upon row*
> *Across the stone steps*
> *And the Temple keys.*

With Mama alternately fluttering and hovering or domineering and demanding, those old ladies opened their purses for the poor Irish poet. My fortune was growing. And I was becoming an indispensable part of Meron House. Seldom now would Mama make a decision without consulting me. She began to show me her own correspondence as a token of the trust between us.

Together, we schemed against Miss Fairweather, or rather against the lady-housekeeper's secret sins which were likely to bring her down into hell. At first by hints, then by open, direct statement Mama intimated to me that she suspected Miss Fairweather, for all that she was a Plymouth Sister, of suffering from pride of the eyes.

Denials that somewhere about the house a pair of curling tongs lay hidden were pointless, because Miss Fairweather often appeared with singed ringlets, though none of us would have dared to mention it. What really worried Mama, more than the worldly, artificial curls themselves, was the use of the electric fire. The lady-housekeeper obviously used the fire in her bedroom to heat the sinful tongs during her afternoon withdrawal, so depriving the starving mission babies of Egypt. What was spent on electric fires could not be spent on saving the heathen. And so Mama and I prayed and schemed.

Eventually a plan was devised. I was stationed one afternoon under Miss Fairweather's bed while she slept. When she woke and got up, I peeped and saw her unlock a drawer and take out the curling tongs. Then she switched on the electric fire. The poor thing almost died from fright when I pounced on her, and flung open the door for a waiting Mama to witness the sin with her own eyes.

It was hard for me to keep from laughing at the absurdity of it all. At the same time, I felt sorry for the pathetic, guilt-stricken housekeeper. I was sorry too, now that the fun was over, to have missed an afternoon on my bicycle, spinning along the autumnal coast. Still, I enjoyed teasing poor Miss Fairweather and compensated any guilt this bred in me by stoutly defending her against the sterner of Mama's anti-sin campaigns.

Miss Fairweather's curls always brought Mama back to 'the Oscar Wilde trouble'. Hans was responsible for this. Many years before, the young German student had stayed with Mama. A housemaid found a hair-net under Han's pillow and with wonder and trembling reported the matter. Mama's voice went diminuendo when the German's hair-net was mentioned. Yet, she would add perplexedly, he had been such a *nice* young man and had played Brahms so beautifully on the drawing-room piano.

There was another nice young man who, although utterly different from Hans, also failed to pass Mama's strict tests, and this was Billy Graham. She decidedly disapproved of new phrases he introduced to the evangelical platform. 'May the Lord bless you real good' was not in the best literary taste and carried overtones of warmth. Warmth was a forbidden emotion.

But Billy Graham's real crime in Mama's eyes was being an American. Her dislike of the United States was not a simple case of prejudice but a considered opinion based on observation of her niece's husband who was an American. Nobody should have been surprised that the ugly word 'divorce' was brought into the family through such an unwise if not exactly ungodly tie-up with the United States. Mama was burdened with the certainty that her niece could never be happy, for the man was a waster. Only once had he been to Meron House and that was more than enough. During the picnic lunch on the beach the man had balanced buttered rolls on his knees, *directly on his trousers and without a plate.* Mama had been unable to take her eyes off the greasy stains which consequently disfigured the expensive flannel suit.

And if one American could be such a waster, what reason had she to suppose that there were not millions of others. And whatever one might think of Billy Graham's evangelizing, he *was*, undeniably, an American. A worse indictment against wasters and a salutary warning about marrying one, came from no less a person than Laura Bell. She had been burdened by her marriage to a spendthrift. Captain Thistlethwayte, her husband, had been in the habit of summoning servants by firing pistol shots into the ceiling. Mama was not disturbed so much by the rather unorthodox manner of calling a servant, as by the waste of bullets.

Mama discovered eventually that, as she suspected, Billy Graham was no better than her niece's husband. In fact, the famous soul-saver was worse because he suffered from the same complaint as Miss Fairweather—the pride of the eyes. Although Mama had always thought it, earlier doubts were confirmed when she saw the facts in print. The blue-eyed evangelist's secret was out. Most of his time at home was spent wearing a green baseball cap so that his blond waves could be kept in perfect order for his Bible campaigns.

Billy Graham's baseball cap and other incidents of minor importance were the rare, glory-clad peaks in the desert of the two ladies' lives. In some obscure, masochistic way Miss Fairweather probably enjoyed being dominated by Mama and teased to the point of torment by me. The lady-housekeeper quickly forgave me about the tongs. Indeed, shortly afterwards she suggested that my hair was too straight for a poet and that I ought to have a go with the tongs myself. Miss Fairweather's feeling towards me and her concern about my hair were it was true, engendered by a good deed of mine. I had put the lady-housekeeper out of her life's greatest agony by letting her know how much Mama would be leaving her in the will.

The pride of the eyes was a sin to be watched for daily. Mama trod constantly on Old Nick's tail to stop him from luring me and other lesser Christians by vanity from that gate and way which were straight and narrow respectively, and which led, albeit thinly populated, unto life. A long mirror hung in the hall at Meron House. Should Mama see my covert glances at myself, glances which tended on the whole to be divided equally in an adolescent way between swooning self-admiration or violent self-criticism, she would give me a gentle rebuke, 'You mustn't be like the Lady Beatrice'.

Indeed no, one must not be like the Lady Beatrice. Although I knew that the Lady Beatrice had been the wife of a most godly rector, she had always gazed at herself in the hall's long mirror. It may have been that this lady wanted to assure herself that she looked more or less in general terms like anybody else and had not gone blue in the face or had grown two heads, because her husband must have been tiresome to live with. At the penny-readings he could quote the whole of *In Memoriam* from memory. If he was like that in public, what must he have been like in private? The Lady Beatrice could hardly be blamed after one visit to her sister in London, for returning to Wales with what was either an elaborate hair-do or a wig.

The Lady Beatrice was already dead before my advent at Meron House. But her memory was evergreen and Mama always experienced a twinge of remorse when we went to Rendezvous Corner. It was there that she had seen the Lady Beatrice's husband, Canon Stewart, for the last time. And with death's awful finality what Mama did then could never be put right. At least, not in this world. Mama hid behind the bushes to avoid the Canon. He was apt to turn the most incidental exchange of 'good mornings' into an excuse for a performance of *In Memoriam*. Mama never forgave herself because she had failed to be 'a channel of blessing' by giving in to this form of pride and evading the Canon.

God's finger touched him, and he slept, and in due course the Lady Beatrice followed her husband into the grave. Her sister in London, however, remained very much alive and was so when I went to Meron House. Unfortunately, the Dowager Lady Tredegar suffered from a pride far worse than the Lady

Beatrice's ocular version. So afflicted, in fact, was Lady Tredegar, that Mama would whisper to me in the most solemn tone that Lady Tredegar was even 'queerer' than Uncle Willie. And for Mama, to be 'queerer' than Uncle Willie was to be queer indeed.

I had to agree that this poor creature's behaviour lay beyond even the field of eccentricity which I accepted as normal at Meron House. Did not Lady Tredegar have monstrous-sized birds' nests built by her own beak and claw in all the rooms of her large London house. And did she not sit on them for hours hatching the eggs underneath, firmly convinced that she was a bird?

Definitely queer. But then this woman's husband, the old lord, had also behaved most 'queerly' when Aunt Mabel went to Tredegar Park with its kangaroos that knocked guests over. That was one country house where I was not encouraged to go, for if Lady Tredegar was 'queer' what was her son Evan? Mama had seen a photograph of Evan Morgan dressed up in frills and ruffs. 'Page to the Pope indeed,' she would snort.

CHAPTER IX

Prisoners

When I first went to live at Meron House, Mama had decided what was to happen if ever the minions of Rome should besiege the house in an attempt to seize my person. The operations had been drawn up in a thorough and military manner, for Mama was utterly convinced that Roman Catholic plans were afoot for my abduction. During those first weeks I was never allowed to answer the telephone in case the Jesuit vassals in Bournemouth were on the line. Neither was I allowed to sit facing the drawing-room windows in case Archbishop McGrath or his snipers were hidden in the rhododendrons taking stock of the situation.

On one famous day, Miss Fairweather came back from the greengrocers inarticulate with terror. Seated and sufficiently calmed, she related what she had just seen at Rendezvous Corner. The lady-housekeeper's tiny, penguin steps had never twittered so rapidly up to the front door before. She had seen a Roman Catholic priest loitering in the gardens at Rendezvous Corner. Poor Miss Fairweather, she was fond of me, and now that it looked as if my hour had come and I was about to be kidnapped, and put in irons and loaded with chains in some monastery dungeon, she went to pieces.

Not so Mama. She immediately seized control of the situation. The house was locked up. Doors and windows were barred. I was sent up to my room and instructed to secure myself in. Then Mama and Miss Fairweather, the one over eighty and the other on the brink of seventy, both rendered almost immobile with rheumatism, took the stoutest umbrellas from the hallstand and went out to investigate the stranger at Rendezvous Corner. But, of course, no assassin was going to await the two ladies' pleasure. Even by the time Mama had got the button-hook for doing her outdoor shoes up, the man had gone. Nevertheless, for days afterwards the main outside door was kept bolted. Only when Mama realized that I could spend whole days in Cardiff without being kidnapped, was the vigilance relaxed.

Yet, when it seemed certain that the Romans had called off their invasion indefinitely, life for the two ladies promised to be unbearably dull. They read *The Churchman's Magazine* every month, and expected one of its stories about converts ruthlessly sought after by 'the Papal Gestapo' to be put in action on the very doorstep of Meron House. But no new excitement promised to relieve their boredom. I hated to see them so low in spirits. It was plain that keeping regular and sleeping with the house-keeping keys were no better than untying the knots in the string-bag on rainy days.

Some of this accidie began to affect me too. A dark night entered my soul. The Latin I was studying turned to ashes in my mouth, for those declensions were no longer spiced by Mama's birdlike and apprehensive glances through the window. In a way I thought I had genuinely failed her by not discovering a priest in the linen cupboard. It began to dawn on me, slowly at first, and then with gathering momentum, what I must do. Just as I had been obliged to create an emergency in order to get a war-time permit to visit Ulster, so now I had to create a kidnapping.

Such a theatrically contrived climax would serve several purposes simultaneously. Mama's boredom would be relieved and her capacity for concentration given something to feed on. Also, Christmas was not far away. Fond though I was of Mama, I did not relish the straightlaced Christmas that Meron House would provide. With increasing desire I thought of my brief, dragon-fly summer-long stay in Bournemouth where I had mixed with the most normal, untwisted people so far encountered since I became 'saved'. I wanted to spend my Christmas with them.

Evangelicals, like some Fleet Street editors, love to send telegrams in Biblical form. Having therefore decided to pass Christmas in Bournemouth I left Meron House one morning and sent Mama a telegram. It contained, simply, the message—Job 3: 25.

Mama's familiarity with the Bible made it unnecessary for her to look up the reference. She knew as well as I that it read, 'For the thing which I greatly feared is come upon me, and that which I was afraid of is come unto me.'

Duly delivered at Meron House, this telegram had the desired galvanizing effect. Emptiness and boredom were things of the past. For Mama and for Miss Fairweather the worst of all possible evils had befallen them. With no doubts of any kind they were sure that the Jesuit Gestapo had captured me at last. I could imagine the two ladies reconstructing the whole drama and cherishing the telegram as evidence of my last minutes of freedom.

Compared with run-of-the-mill evangelicals, and especially compared with the religious extremists of the Bible Academy, Mama's anti-Catholic ideas were not violent. Her principal objection to Rome was its irreverent attitude to the Lord's Day. Apparently the Church of Rome cared nothing for the proper observance of Sunday. Also, Mama considered it lacking in civilized decorum for them to keep making references in their Hail Marys to a certain part of the female body. *Blessed is the fruit of thy womb* was something which poor Mama could not abide, the effect on her was pathological. But even this was not a super-sensitiveness to Roman ways for Mama would not even read her solid Protestant *Daily Bread* notes aloud with me if the day's passage from the Bible contained naughty words. The worst word of all, even worse than 'womb' was 'circumcision'. Mama's obsession about circumcision was greater than the Bible's own. It was not nice and Mama felt ill if the word was used.

However, for the Christmas holidays I had left all that behind me, and settled once more comfortably and happily at
Bournemouth in St. Joseph's Convent. I waited a few days
before sending Mama my address. I was just about to leave the
building on my way to a New Year dance in one of Bournemouth's smart hotels, when somebody said there was a telephone call for me. Reverend Mother stripped the tall telephone
of its tea-cosy to connect me with the equally tall mouth-piece
in Meron House.

I heard Miss Fairweather's ladylike 'Are you there?' Nothing
so common for her as the 'hallo' of Aunt Mabel's working-
housekeeper. When I assured Miss Fairweather that I *was* there,
she handed over to Mama. She was more distressed than I had
thought possible. My kidnapping prank had deeply upset her.
Had it been possible, Mama would have left Meron House
there and then to come to Bournemouth and rescue me. All
that prevented her was the thought that the routine of Meron
House would collapse without her presence. What, for instance,
would happen if Violet should take it into her head not to come
home after her café wanderings while her mother was in
Bournemouth?

But if Mama could not come in person to rescue me, then
some of her 'fellow-warriors at the Throne of Grace' could, and
in fact did. Significantly, another of Mama's favourite missionary societies kept an office in Bournemouth. And the Prayer
Secretary and Junior Partners Secretary lived at the Christian
hotel at Boscombe. Further to this, also at the hotel was no less
a notable than Percival Petter, better known to evangelicals as
the founder of the National Union of Protestants, but who with
his twin brother designed and built the first internal combus-
tion motor-car engine in England.

Percival Petter had recently earned himself another sort of
fame by staging demonstrations at the enthronement of Dr.
Wand, in St. Paul's Cathedral, as Bishop of London. Now,
Percival devoted his attention to getting me out of St. Joseph's
Convent. None of these diehard Protestants could believe that
I was staying at the convent voluntarily. To satisfy their own

lust for self-importance they *had* to believe that the Catholics were holding me by force.

A dilemma now arose. I could stay on at St. Joseph's, of course, but it was becoming increasingly embarrassing with the Protestant people always pestering. Also, Mama continued to be upset by the situation. As I had only intended to spend Christmas at Bournemouth, I thought it might be just as well to leave as more or less planned. Though in later years it was possible to look back and be scathing about the puffed-up self-importance of the Protestant brigade, I was also full of my own importance. At seventeen I could never resist the opportunity of investing life with a dramatic value it did not possess in reality. Faced with the possibility of new excitements, and also with the chance of quieting poor Mama's soul, I played up to the Petter people.

On the whole, I made a bad bargain in exchanging St. Joseph's Convent for the Christian hotel at Boscombe, in giving up the comparative freedom of the one for the crabbed bigotry of the other. So convinced were my Protestant defenders that the Jesuits were still after me that I was registered at the Christian hotel under the assumed name of Charles Stafford. Although all the people at the hotel were active Christian workers my identity was kept secret from all but a few. Nobody was told my reason for being in the place. Night and morning they allowed me to take exercise outside the hotel like a dog.

During the day I continued, somewhat erratically, with my studies, tutored by an old clergyman who trudged miles every day to do so. I could not go to him in case I was spotted by the Sacred Heart crowd. Again, rumours went round that the hotel was being watched by Jesuit priests.

What I had intended as a joke on Mama, had developed into a major situation in my life. Short of running away, there seemed no solution. Then to relieve the siege came the suggestion that I should go to the Tyndale Training College in London, where the Tyndale Preachers had their headquarters. Anything being better than Boscombe, I agreed, thinking that in London I would be able to take a broader view of what I was aiming to do with my life. For at this time there was still no doubt that in one form or another yet to be discovered, my life was to be spent doing the Lord's work.

The Tyndale Training College was run by the strictest, most puritanical apostle of evangelism imaginable. The Bournemouth people considered it the best establishment for me to train in. The utmost vigilance was kept right up until the moment of my departure from the Christian hotel. To avoid Jesuit plotters who might have caught wind of the new plans— who might have spies waiting for me at Bournemouth's main station—I was driven out of town to catch the train at a smaller station. One of the Tyndale Preachers took charge of me there. And he was the man who, before we even got to Waterloo station had turned my stomach against the Tyndale Training College.

We had a compartment to ourselves and sat opposite each other by the window. The other man's entire conversation consisted solely of tirades against the Roman Catholic Church and Anglo-Catholic abuses also rife in Bournemouth. He peered into the seamy-side of life and by so doing revealed not the so-called corruptions of the Roman religion but the sordid state of his own mind. He horrified and repulsed me by his own special argument against transubstantiation. To prove his point he opened his Bible and extracted a white disc from its leaves. I thought it was a cardboard imitation of a Communion wafer. He held it out for my inspection and explained that it was, in fact, the Blessed Sacrament itself, consecrated and laid in good faith by a priest on the man's own tongue. He had taken Communion at a Mass under false pretences, removing the consecrated wafer from his mouth afterwards. Was this, he laughed, fingering the wafer coarsely, Our Lord's body?

The man was revolting. It was not that at this period in my life I was persuaded one way or the other about Roman Catholic doctrine. The actual mechanics of transubstantiation seemed irrelevant. The point was, that to the people who took this sacrament the bread was sacred. And as far as I could tell from my long talks with various Catholics, both clergy and laity, all they wanted was that this bread and its wine should also become sacred to me. But here was this disgusting little man dragging other people's cherished loves through the mire of his own dirty mind.

He was a type I had met so often in evangelical circles, not merely narrow but actively replusive. Anything of beauty, anything of warmth or emotional attachment or even plain, animal pleasure was translated into a degrading filthiness. Their own ambience was cold like their houses, their thoughts without loveliness. By contrast, the Catholics had enveloped me with not a little humanity charged with warmth by a God, it seemed, who was radically different from the evangelical one. I loathed the Tyndale Preacher for his vulgarity and brutality of spirit. Before reaching London I had resolved to make my stay with his society a short one.

My journey from the Christian hotel to the Tyndale Training College culminated in meeting the Principal. His claim to fame lay in the fact that his father had been famous in Victorian times as an iconoclast who passed much of his time, not in rest and quietness, but in smashing crucifixes and other symbols of popery in Anglican churches. His son spent several hours looking me over and then took me to a room in the college's student wing. For entertainment he left me a stack of pamphlets.

I was told to pay special attention to a leaflet which made short work of papal blessing. I lay in the dull little room out at North Harrow going over the list of papal blessings which, of course, turned and rended the recipients, proving not to be blessings at all, but curses and disaster. But what were such things to me? I had taken more than enough of such purgatives in my time, beginning in my evacuee days in Fermanagh with the equally obnoxious little book *How We Differ from Rome,* which I had to learn off by heart before I could be confirmed.

Of what possible importance could it be to me that Princess Ena had forsaken her Protestant faith to marry a Catholic King of Spain with the result that her 'wedding garments were bespattered with human blood'. A still-not-completely-tamed Irish youth like myself could feel no pangs that General

Boulanger had committed suicide after receiving the papal blessing or that the 'charity' bazaar in Paris went up in flames destroying 'nearly 150 of the aristocracy' because the Papal Nuncio had given the affair his blessing.

I put the stupid pamphlet aside and gazed at the prospect of North Harrow through the window. Then I stood up. I wanted London lights and noise and the swirl of blood in the veins. Protestants and Catholics alike could go to hell, or to heaven, for all I was concerned. Tyndale Training College was colder and narrower than even the Bible Academy and I saw what a poor exchange I had made. The idea of going to such a place had attracted me for I thought it would be one more stepping-stone in my ambitious crossing from poverty to security. I hated it and sadly missed the comforting Victorian twilight of Meron House. Quaint and eccentric though Mama was, she had given me the security I wanted so much. I missed her love too and loathed every hard, harsh thing about Tyndale Training College and its Protestant primitiveness.

I had to get out of the place, away from the smell of sin scrubbed with carbolic. At St. Joseph's I had been able to dissipate at least some of the heat of youth's high temperature. The company of normal girls and boys of my own age in Bournemouth where we went swimming or to dances had shown me that explosive reactions against the repressive effects of pseudo-piety were not necessary. Yet here I was, almost exploding again in the Protestant lair at North Harrow.

My problem became the immediate one of where to go in London so late in the evening. But I certainly had no intention of being tucked up with anti-Roman pamphlets. This would almost certainly produce in me the same effect which papal blessing had on General Boulanger—suicide.

It was too late to call on the Misses Curry, my usual London contacts when I had gone up from Meron House. In any case these ladies were strong supporters of the Tyndale Training College which, like so many evangelical institutions, later received a substantial chunk from their estate. The only person who had said that I was more than welcome to call on him literally at any hour out of a day's twenty-four was the Lady Beatrice's nephew, Lord Tredegar.

There was about Evan's outrageousness something magnificent. There was no meanness of spirit in it at all. Fascinating too was the way he flouted the conventions of society while paradoxically preserving them meticulously in his person. Evan was a master-craftsman of living. He was one of the last great Bohemians. Blessed with wealth and the temperament for its full enjoyment, Evan surrounded himself with beauty and learning. He kept beautiful men-servants and an array of pet animals. He endeavoured to ensure that whatever he looked upon or heard or touched was beautiful. In this he was more like a High Renaissance prince than a papal courtier of the twentieth century.

Evan's mother, clucking and brooding in her Grosvenor Square nests, could not compare in terms of the bizarre with his own black magic circles or after-theatre orgies. He was capable of having a royal tea-party cancelled if some obscure actor telephoned him and wanted Evan's time and money immediately to get him out of trouble. In spite of wealth's various temptations Evan never fell into the vice of idleness. He painted well, or badly enough, to have canvases hung in the Paris Salon. He also played musical instruments and had several books of his poetry published. And to satisfy the wide curiosity of his mind and his catholic taste he collected *objets d'art* and human beings. If Tredegar Park reflected his great love of the Italian Renaissance, his London home echoed to the screech of everything new and vital in religion and the arts.

I was seventeen years old. To be faced with the choice between the drabness of the Tyndale Training College at North Harrow or the gilded splendour of Lord Tredegar's house left me with no qualms. Who would prefer the Tyndale Preachers' calculated misery to Evan's *joie de vivre*?

Evan chuckled to the nearest parrot and while I made myself comfortable in a voluptuously padded chair, a young footman handed me a stiff drink. Its alcoholic content, I thought, was hardly strong enough to wash away all the sins of evangelism I had committed in the past few weeks. Evan remarked how tall I was growing, and if, he said, we were going to make the Ritz, I had better change into some other clothes. He was sure they would fit me. So instead of studying Protestant railleries against papal blessings, I tried on the dress clothes of the Papal Chamberlain. Then I went to try out on the Ritz menu the French imparted by Mama.

French, I was finding, was by no means a foible of Mama's. In Evan's world it was important. It flowed as musically as the Welsh I had heard in the valleys on my caravan mission. And it seemed to be used for expressing the subtle things of a life unknown to me until I went to Meron House. How could you order wine in anything but a French accent? No such thing as *pâté de foie gras* existed in English. *Le Roi Soleil* was quite another thing than Louis the Fourteenth—the one was a king of the sun, the other a mere name in a boring list of royalty.

Although I was no connoisseur like Evan, I began to glimpse the broad sunlit landscapes of the cultured life. Though still gauche, I began to envy those people who had taste. The power to discriminate, to select one luxury rather than another, to plump for this kind of sensory and sensual experience rather than that, appeared to me as more likely to save the soul than any other method. Instead of the narrow, poverty-stricken language of evangelicals, I heard strange, new consonances in Italian and German and in French, each word a hint of something I had yet to discover. It no longer seemed heathen that Roman Catholics should choose to shield their mysteries in a language reserved for that sole purpose. I thought it only right that my extraordinary friend Evan should have left England a private secretary to the Parliamentary Secretary of the Minister of Labour to become Privy Chamberlain of the Sword and Cape, to the Pope.

I, a gangling youth who had once had his cards in at a Belfast shipbuilding firm, now thought the Ministry of Labour an institution of philistines. Because of Evan I walked through the fields of heaven reaping stardust. But the more my sickle went among the golden grain, the more I saw waving just out of my reach. And beyond, horizon followed horizon.

When I thought of how I had preached in Irish farm cottages, I blushed. I considered myself pretty smart, pretty well-up in knowing what there was to know about what was worth knowing. When I remembered the Welsh valleys now, my blush deepened. How many times had I thought myself so superior to those country folk because I had crossed the Water from Ireland and could tell them a thing or two about the world beyond their dry-stone walls? And how many times had I talked about 'soul'? Now, although I still thought it a good thing, on the whole, to have one's soul saved, I was no longer sure what the soul was anyway, let alone how to save it. Evan's black magic, evoked by the skeleton hand of a famous Welsh witch, intrigued me more than the beautiful rosary (specially blessed by the Pope, of course!) he had given me.

And so, by the progression by which adolescence changes into manhood, I found another sort of black magic even more exciting than Evan's variety. That I thought of it as black magic hardly mattered since George Gurdjieff himself liked to be called the Devil. I wanted to be the Devil's disciple, and dreamt enviously of those Parisian vodka sessions in his flat on the Rue des Colonels Rénards.

Things went on there, I was sure, for which there was no adequate expression in English, not even the devouring of music in which Gurdjieff resembled Evan. Perhaps, in view of the Master's own ideas, it was not in the least extraordinary that it should have been Biddy O'Brien in one of the Fermanagh farm cottages which I knew as an evacuee, who should lead me to Gurdjieff.

Biddy O'Brien could neither read nor write. And since even among the chalky hills of Fermanagh to be capable of both became an inescapable necessity, I acted as scribe to Biddy on such occasions when the new-fangled world intruded on her time-immemorial ways. Years before, while she was a serving-girl, Biddy had given birth to a 'wee love-bird' who was called Tommy and who grew to be a man, much, perhaps, like any other man. He went as a soldier in the war and this was the cause of my scribing, for his mother Biddy wrote to him and eventually her thoughts and my handwriting were trickling through to the Far East where Tommy had become a prisoner-of-war with the Japanese, and an existentialist.

When I left Fermanagh to put my cards in the shipyard and to make my fortune on Queen's Island, I forgot about Biddy and her son Tommy, except occasionally when I indulged in fond memories of how she had written that her pullets were laying or that the rats were at her potato-pit again, or that the pig-sticker was dead or the byreman had got married at last; apart from this I forgot them both. Then years later, before my brief stay with the Tyndale Preachers came to its unlamented end, I learnt that Tommy was living in Bedford. I got his address and arranged to meet him when he came to London for a prisoner-of-war reunion. What wheels there were within wheels. That meeting with Tommy was to cost me two considerable fortunes, and was to lead to Meron House closing its doors against me, just as those same doors had been bolted in defiance and terror against the priests of Rome.

Tommy and his friends showed me an unsuspected horizon. How far away now Biddy O'Brien's kitchen seemed with its *ceili* round the fire and its cowslip tea. Yet when I looked again long afterwards, I saw that Biddy knew all along what life was about. But she was too simple for a clever fellow like me.

Tommy and the other returned prisoners-of-war still had a parchment look about them. Their tropical experiences still surrounded them with its horror and humour. What surprised me was to hear them talking now about the cosmic laws of three and seven (shades of Evan who loved things in threes and who left a residue of his millions to Buckfast Abbey monks so that they would say a Mass once very seven days for seven years after his death), and about the Master in Paris, Gurdjieff, and about the group in Sloane Street and the centre in Ipswich. I was making my first Gurdjieff contact. Where it would lead did not concern me. I enjoyed the company of these young soldiers who seemed to speak of a new life, a new forgiveness:

Prisoners

We are come out of a strange land
Into the light.
There is no grudge.
Can the moon hate the sun
For his power and heat?
We had the sun then on our faces
Out of a full sky.
Hot, fierce, unwelcome almost
Its light; intensely dark and
Revealing in brilliance strange
Unfriendly shapes we did not know,
Or could not, for our hearts
Did not grasp at them out of our bodies
To make them part of ourselves.
The rocks we walked on
And the trees our hopeful fingers touched
Did not become one with us
By the blessing of our presence.
They remained, alone
Unbefriended in the blinded sun.

CHAPTER X

Dandelions and the Rape

❧❦❧

Never before had grace been said over drawing-room tea at Meron House. An event of catastrophic scale was needed to bring this unprecedented performance, which thereafter sometimes included singing the Keswick grace.

I was home again from the spiritual wars and secular wonders of London, home safely behind the starched net curtains through which the weak Welsh sunlight was filtered on to Mama's tea-tray. When I returned to the house after my odyssey, I felt a pang that my high spirits had caused Mama such agonies. When she put her crippled fingers into mine and implored me not to rush into rash behaviour and to settle down to my studies at least until my eighteenth birthday, I realized that I had become extremely fond of Mama, and that in a curious and quite unexpected way I had missed her during my adventures in Bournemouth and London.

Even when she made herself ridiculous by standing on the balcony and beseeching the Holy Ghost to give pin-pricks to her pride, or when she stood wrapped in a Shetland shawl awaiting the return of the housekeeping keys, I could not help being drawn to her. She had taken me to her heart. I was the grandson she pined for. And Mama spoilt me as she had never spoilt her own children. She confided matters to me which would never have been mentioned to the others.

Temporarily sated with excitement I allowed the quiet of Meron House to embalm me. Without a rumble of protest I submitted to Mama's advice and opened my books once again. Secretly I was glad, for the house gave me a sense of security and I liked this, at least for a time. Mama was a sensible woman in spite of her eccentricities. She realized that a lusty young fellow of seventeen could not rest long content with no company other than antimacassars and maiden ladies. So she scouted round the neighbourhood's large houses and provided me with companions of my own age, with whom I could go swimming and boating during the weeks following my return.

I did not find these young people as tiresome as I might have done a few months previously, and no doubt the reverse was also true. The urge to go and indulge myself in Bute Town had not abated. But the sophistication associated with such matters in London had momentarily put me off the coarser aspects of Bute Town. So I swam and boated and took drawing-room tea with my young friends. For Mama, these arrangements had only one flaw. Not all the young friends were 'washed in the blood'.

Mama's fears were not that these unsaved boys would corrupt me, but rather that a fine opportunity of bringing some young souls to the Lord was slipping by. Fortunately, Mama had never allowed herself to become obsessed with the indiscriminate handing out of Gospel tracts. Perhaps also she feared in this case that if I was embarrassed by an excessive display of evangelical zeal, I would take myself off to the Roman camp again. So we dispensed with propriety and said grace over afternoon tea.

This concession made no difference, of course, to the routine by which Meron House had been ruled since its foundation. Grace at drawing-room tea made no variation to the law that Monday's luncheon, as well as Sunday's was cold. Both Mama and Miss Fairweather visited the chiropodist on Mondays. Also on Mondays, the kitchen was completely occupied like a field of battle by the Austrian Frau and her army of washing mounted on horses and suspended by pulleys like medieval knights about to be lowered on to their chargers.

The mercy of God would certainly not protect any interloper among the Monday laundry. It was not even certain that the Almighty would Himself have been admitted because Mama's rules for the washing were omnipotent. The laundry had to be watched far more closely than even the wastage on Miss Fairweather's potato peelings. Wool principally occupied Mama's attention. In her opinion, wool which did not come from Scotland was simply not wool at all. Consequently all the vests and combinations came from Edinburgh. It was the Frau's duty to see that the woollens went through the correct drying procedure. Lamentations heaped themselves upon this poor woman should Mama discover a pair of woollen drawers on a horse near the fire. The woollens had to leap from horse to horse, starting at the back and advancing by degrees nearer the glowing range. If ever Monday's woollens should be found anywhere near the fire before Tuesday afternoon at the earliest, a long sermon followed by a tense atmosphere fell on the poor Austrian woman.

Similar scruples applied to the Lord's Day itself, and to Saturday's preparations. Although man was not made for the Sabbath, in Meron House he had to be somewhat less of a man than on any other day. Mama, for instance, would not think of ordering the car for Sunday morning. No matter how painful her arthritis was, she hobbled from Meron House to the nearest mission hall in the morning. In the evening she listened to the service on the wireless, unaware that a score or so of engineers were actually working on the Lord's Day in order to put out the broadcast.

Miss Fairweather came into the drawing-room to hear the service. This was the only time in the week when the lady-housekeeper actually sat in the drawing-room. And to show that this was a privilege as opposed to a right of duty, she did not have to surrender the keys, although she sat clutching them tightly. When the wireless service finished and the ancient set was switched off a pause followed. Properly speaking, Miss Fairweather should have risen then and gone about her ways. But this never happened, because she and Mama were waiting for me to begin.

Dandelions and the Rape

Both women, frail and tiny, sat on the edge of the chairs, their eyes fixed childlike on mine, waiting for me to begin. And I would not have hurt them more by cutting their heads off than I would have done by not telling them a Sunday story. The stories had to be about my earlier life in Ireland. It was always fantastic and never quite real to them, this wild, romantic, impossibly beautiful Ireland.

On most Sunday evenings I found no difficulty in finding tales to keep the old ladies in suspense and terror or fits of laughter. Their own lives had been humdrum for so many years that almost any other form of existence seemed exotic by comparison. It seemed wonderful to them that I had eaten smoked badger or had divined wells with hazel rods. After five minutes of my Sunday story neither of them remembered what the preacher had said in his broadcast.

The Sunday tales were never allowed to finish without a climax, preferably about a bull or the breaking of a young horse. Both Mama and Miss Fairweather went rigid with terror at the thought of being chased and tossed by a bull. It haunted the lady-housekeeper's life to the extent that she never wore red nor any shade of red. How she expected to encounter a mad bull along the seafront promenade or at Rendezvous Corner and the public park where nothing fiercer than pekineses were ever seen, I never understood. But by relating quite ordinary things which I remembered about bulls, the two old ladies could be sent cold and sweating to their beds to be chased until daylight by many-horned bulls foaming at the mouth.

Mama and Miss Fairweather loved it. The Sunday climax became essential and made addicts of them. The two ladies could no more have gone without their stimulant than if they had both been opium smokers. Eventually I ran out of true stories and had to invent episodes which began with mad bulls of inconceivable strength bursting from their pens and charging helpless women who had to save themselves by leaping fully-clothed into rivers.

One Sunday evening tale resulted in drastic and unfortunate

141

effects on Miss Fairweather who was frightened as much by earwigs as by mad bulls. She knew that earwigs could go through the human ear into the brain. When I told her and Mama about an old supersition concerning earwigs the poor lady-housekeeper never afterwards relaxed, especially not in the gardens or at Rendezvous Corner whose overhanging bushes, I assured her, hung heavy with earwigs. The superstition held that when an earwig was killed, its mate sought the killer and crawled into his or her brain as revenge.

Miss Fairweather's knowledge of natural history was so scanty that she could believe in anything she heard, so that a new terror now came permanently to stalk her. A great clump of pinks grew by the front door and a colony of earwigs lived under it. Miss Fairweather had been in the habit of lifting up the flowers which hung over the garden path to crush the earwigs with the bottom of a milk bottle. Now, when she heard that at sundown the widowed mates set out, stopping at nothing, to find the criminal, the mass-murderer lady-housekeeper almost went into hysterics. What of the victims squashed by the hundreds on empty milk bottles left out every morning? What of those who perished ignominiously in floods of boiling water? How many revenging earwigs must there be trying to enter the house and reach Miss Fairweather's room, doubtless in the dead of night? The idea filled her with such horror that for weeks afterwards she kept cotton wool in her ears. Until the end of her life she never went into the garden or along to Rendezvous Cornc without the cotton wool ear-plugs, making a curious sight together with the green eye-shade she wore, sun or no sun, out of doors.

Months went by which were almost an idyll for me. Time was pleasantly shared between books and friends and my adopted Mama and her lady-housekeeper. Then one morning Miss Fairweather passed along the corridor to Mama's room to collect the keys earlier than usual, braving Violet's displeasure. I could hear her get a cane-bottomed chair and climb cautiously on to it to reach the top shelves of Mama's wardrobe. She was getting out a pile of wrapped parcels which would go downstairs and be placed on the dining-room table amid a froth of greenery and flowers. It was my eighteenth birthday.

Many visitors called in the afternoon, each of them with a gift, for Mama seldom spoke to any of her friends nowadays without praising her beloved Roberto who had brought such pleasure at an unexpected, late moment in her life. The visitors included an old Quaker woman who had been headmistress of the preparatory school where Mama's son had gone. Before the woman left Meron House it was decided that I would do well to teach in a similar school.

Mama opposed the idea at first, but agreed with good grace when she realized that I could not spend my whole life strolling up to Rendezvous Corner with her or in pruning the roses. And since Mama was convinced that I no longer wished to train for the mission field, schoolmastering, she supposed, was not a bad alternative. In all this, Mama never imagined anything but that she would continue living and live long enough to see my career, whatever that was to be, well on its way. She took it for granted that she would long outlast her own mother's ninety-six years, and she almost did despite her cruel arthritis.

For Mama to agree that I could teach was one thing, but her agreement as to how a teaching job should be obtained was another. We could not consult anything quite so vulgar as a London agency. Apart from this being undignified, there was the possibility that such an agency might place me in a crank school. And so Aunt Mabel's latest copy of the *Methodist Recorder* was fetched and its charges for advertisements noted and a suitable one written out for publication in the paper.

Replies were coming in to Meron House within a week, for this was 1946 when teachers were in short supply. The situation in many places was so desperate that some schools offered posts immediately without an interview.

However, Caroline College for the Daughers of Gentlefolk did ask for my photograph, before urging me to join them post-haste in Somerset. The possession or otherwise of academic qualifications took second place to the possession of sound social references, with which I was now equipped, having some signatures out of the top drawer.

I liked the idea of Somerset and also of the genteel Daughters though it was for the college boys' department I was wanted. Mama had no doubts that I ought to go, in spite of Caroline College being a pronouncedly Anglican establishment run by two elderly sisters, the Misses Grey-Moffat. The saving grace was the senior mistress who was a Methodist and had therefore seen my advertisement in *The Recorder*. Further, this same lady commended herself in Mama's eyes by being the scion of the good and solid if not well-known Cornish family of Nance-Trelawny.

With Mama's blessings heaped on me I set off in high hopes for Somerset and was not disappointed when a hired car from the station took me through magnificent parkland standing among succulent, strawberry-tea landscapes found only in Somerset. By rights, these magnificent, spacious grounds should have been the setting of a house of equal merit. This was unfortunately not the case, though the elder Miss Grey-Moffat was at pains to remind her pupils that the architectural dishabille of the place was considerably compensated by the fact that most of the Hanoverian royalty had either dined or stayed in the house.

Departed grandeur of this kind was of little help, however, in the present circumstances. I had no consolation in thinking about Georgian orgies of gross overeating and drinking and wenching in the banqueting hall. All that worried me was to try and hold a class of nine-year-olds in one corner of the banqueting hall while interrupting maids tried with equal difficulty to set the rows of tables for the first sitting of luncheon.

Oddities of this kind, I soon found, were normal at Caroline College. I managed to preserve an appearance of superior calm when I discovered that some of the boys in the supposed preparatory school department were only a year or so younger than myself. And nothing proved to be quite so odd as my first morning when, halfway through it, the door burst open and in came a strange, beautiful creature who turned out to be Miss

Dailes, the English mistress. From beneath the wildly-escaping, prematurely white hair two Ophelia-like eyes peered at me. A well modulated voice begged me to take the Ovaltine tablets which she offered, for teaching exhausted the nerves so. She was right, of course, especially teaching in its context of Caroline College, but I thought her behaviour eccentric, to say the least. Poor Miss Dailes, she later became permanently resident in a mental hospital.

I thought many times, both then and afterwards, how she resembled Hamlet's Ophelia, and how, in the same way, she was more tragic than that self-torturing youth. Myrtle Dailes's tragedy, like Ophelia's, was the poignant tragedy of madness enshrined in beauty.

For the moment, however, Myrtle installed herself as my faithful watch-dog. Mad or not, she made it her business to see that the horrors of teaching did a minimum of damage to my supposedly susceptible nature.

Following the morning's interruption of my class, I found Myrtle in my room in the evening. She was lying on my bed when I went in. Miss Dailes looked at me rather as an artist might look at his model. Clearly, for Myrtle, it was not *my* room, but *a* room, the room in which fortune had decreed I should live, the room to which my opening, morning eyes adjusted themselves either with the rising of the sun or the ringing of the alarm clock, whichever was the earlier.

Myrtle Dailes projected her own existence into mine. At the time I did not understand empathy. When I found Myrtle stretched full-length on my bed, alternately opening and closing her eyes so that she could vicariously enjoy the experience I had on waking each morning, I decided that she was well on the way to complete madness. Myrtle Dailes was in love with me. She identified her own being with mine, and the intensity of experience eventually overwhelmed her completely.

But I saw in later years that it was no madness for Miss Dailes to trespass the borders of normal behaviour if she felt herself peculiarly sensitive to whatever touched me. But at eighteen I was either too brutal, or too terrified, to accept the implications, and besides, Myrtle embarrassed me. Almost every day, after that first evening when I discovered her on my bed, she left notes under my pillow. Although they said nothing of importance, I was too blind to sympathize with the force of feeling which produced them. It was not, after all, the sort of expression in which Mama would have indulged.

It was sad that love was subject to the pressure of practical affairs, for in coping with this aspect of things Myrtle failed dismally. Through the innocent medium of the *Methodist Recorder* I had got myself a job and it had to be done. Whatever importance Myrtle may have attached to arithmetic and parsing she should at least have recognized that, for the moment at least, I was honour bound to teach these things to the best of my ability. As it was, during my classes showers of notes would arrive by pupil messengers, each of which had to be opened and read to the detriment of such matters as that the Iberian peninsula was composed of Spain and Portugal and British Gibraltar or that the sum of the parts could not be greater than the whole.

Myrtle's written interruptions eventually became such a nuisance that I had to speak sharply to her. But the tears which formed in those beautiful blue eyes were only a further intoxicant to a woman already drunk with love. Thereafter, I might be writing Latin exercises in chalk when through the open window a blackboard pointer would appear with yet another note pinned to its end.

Among Myrtle's fantasies was a belief that in a former existence she had been a seal-woman. Her illusion had a curious beauty like the Swan-maiden of Germany or the Seal-woman of the Faroes. Unfortunately for her, the young man on whom she fastened her attention was trying his best to be everything which a prep schoolmaster should be. He found it embarrassing to have the English mistress suddenly appearing from behind a rock on the Somerset coast when he was trying to teach swimming to the younger boys. Every inch a seal-woman, Myrtle would rise from the most improbable corner of a cove just when the boys were at their most intractible, either dressing or

Dandelions and the Rape

undressing. How could I respond with anything but coldness to the Russalka-like pleading in those sea-blue eyes?

Because she was not of this world, Myrtle could not command discipline. Pandemonium reigned in her classroom. And when she took the boy boarders for prep she was overwhelmed. The first thing to be seized was poor Myrtle's bag. This long, embroidered sack held Myrtle's childhood teddy-bear, and stones or pieces of glass picked up on the beach, and the shells of crabs which she had given me. Wound among these curios were old stockings long past the mending stage, out-of-date examinations papers, and her paints and brushes. The boys upended the sack and tumbled its contents on to the floor, on the beach or the cricket field, and held up her treasures to public ridicule. Myrtle, however, had spirit and often wrestled with an offender to retrieve a particular treasure, perhaps a sea-whitened twig she had discovered lodged in the rock where earlier in the day she had concealed her seal-woman's body.

Myrtle suffered all fools without gladness, excepting me. I, in my turn, suffered her because it flattered me to have the attentions of this fey, beautiful woman foisted on me. In the school, her antics merely inconvenienced my teaching, but in the town they actively embarrassed me. Myrtle would come running after me in the street crying, 'Beloved, beloved, I've got the muffins.'

To what depths love will sink to fulfil itself! Muffins! But though I adopted such airs and graces as Mama thought a young man should have, and although I played my part of a master in a rather smart school, I was, nevertheless, still an ever-hungry youth who found the dining-room food well below satisfaction level. Also, the staff seldom wanted their supper at six o'clock so that Myrtle's muffins served with running, melted butter and steaming tea seemed a most sensible expression of love.

Even this comfort was not without worry for Myrtle did the cooking and brewing in her bedroom. I lived in terror of her spirit stoves standing about the chintz-hung room. The lemonade bottles filled with methylated spirit were always being knocked over, and if it were cold, Myrtle carried one of the lighted stoves along the passages to keep her warm in the lavatory.

Myrtle's mind was never quite on her subject during teaching hours for she was then busy scheming how best I might be fed. What had begun on the first morning as Ovaltine tablets ended with soused herrings or melons or lychees and sometimes gargantuan lobsters.

Myrtle's last big fling was the dandelion gathering. At Caroline College the best rooms as well as the main staircase and entrance were reserved for the sole and private use of the Misses Grey-Moffat. They liked to think that the place was still their own home where they could entertain. The two ladies therefore occupied a large portion of the house, while the eighty school staff and boarders were crammed into the servants' wings. All eighty even had to use the same bathroom with its single bath, although this desperate situation was occasionally relieved when some of the senior boys were allowed to use the younger Miss Grey-Moffat's marble bath which was built in her bedroom. Early mornings were not so frantic for me because a maid brought a brass can of hot water to empty into a china bowl as ancient as the one Mama used at Meron House.

Though born both to the manner and its luxuries, the Misses Grey-Moffat were often hard-put-to-it to sustain their way of living. Their cellars, for instance, were depleted and few bottles coated with age and cobwebs remained. For the most, home-made wines constituted the ladies' principal form of hospitality. And it was the children from the school who had to go out collecting the raw material for these wines, first being shown quite clearly which flowers and berries should be picked.

As usual in such schools, the boys and girls belonged to houses, and those at Caroline College were named after Somerset saints. Points were also awarded for good behaviour or work done during each week, resulting in fierce competitions. At the end of the year the house with the most points was awarded the school cup. One way to earn the precious points was on the wine flower and berry collecting days. A hundred rose hips or a hundred elderberry blossoms earned one point. This was not only spendid character training for children who would spend the remainder of their lives picking metaphorical rose hips, but it was also a day when the senior boys and girls could meet without let or hindrance behind the blackberry bushes.

Under these circumstances, then, there was no need for the staff to whip up artificial enthusiasm. The children flung themselves without reserve into the picking and plucking. To Myrtle was given charge over the dandelion department. It was her job to collect the yellow heads from the children and give in return the cards, a blue card for one point, a red card for two points. But the wonder with which thousands of dandelion heads filled Myrtle, quite overcame her sense of duty and she began to scatter them about as though she were God flinging stars into the firmament. The dandelions lay, brilliant and golden on the grass, where they tumbled from the heads and shoulders of the boys upon whom the English mistress had showered them. Being used to Myrtle's antics the boys took it all as a matter of course, even when she began to eat the dandelions, cramming them into her mouth so that a yellow stain appeared round her lips and on her chin.

But Myrtle was not the school's only eccentric, nor was she the worst of characters who tormented the Misses Grey-Moffat by reminders that their home was no longer a stately one. The ladies had more trouble from the kindergarten mistress and the matron than from Myrtle. A scene of distressing vulgarity rent the dignity of Caroline College in twain one morning. It happened before my class was moved out of the dining-room so that I saw the matron join the kindergarten mistress in battle against the younger Miss Grey-Moffat. The matron was a rough-tongued Yorkshire lass with a war-time career as a Land Army girl. The younger principal was made of more rarefied stuff and she did the cooking and the elocution. The clash of temperaments was inevitable and that quarrel about the kindergarten mistress's daughter who was ill, ended all their quarrels. Nothing could separate the three enraged women nor could anyone stop the boys and girls from crowding at the windows to pick up what they could in the way of scandal. And scandal there was in plenty, a whole lot of petty but dirty linen washed in public. The school lawyer, whose brother had been captain on one of Mama's boats, was eventually called in and the matron and kindergarten mistress were dismissed.

Feuds and counter-feuds on matters of the smallest importance kept the staff constantly on the boil. I even had one myself with another Irish master, a man from Dublin who took great exception to a stage-Irish landlady in one of the staff plays which were presented once a term. He thought that the rest of the staff were putting this particular piece on as a deliberate insult to the Irish. He refused to act in it himself and thought I should protest also. But I wanted to be in the play. The Dublin master at first stopped speaking to me and then one night began to fight me. I got two black eyes, he strained his heart and the doctor sent him home to Ireland. Every pupil in the school from the smallest infants whose fathers were still in the Indian Army to the over-bosomy Spanish ladies in the Sixth Form knew how I got my shiners. The boys in my house were extremely proud of them and thought it marvellous that I had to wear sunglasses in December.

When I saw the long crocodiles of boys and girls walking about the town in their smart uniforms, doing precision road-drill, I often wondered how they escaped apparently unharmed from the lunacy of the staff, most of whom stayed for one term only. My own duration of four terms was quite a record in Caroline College. Poor Myrtle Dailes was hardly noticeable in that collection of cranks. And if she should shower house-points on a boy who spat in her face, nobody would take the slightest notice.

Myrtle was among those who stayed only one term. When she had gone I was able to settle down to some teaching. Very quickly I was elevated from the dining-room and given a proper classroom. I also went up from the nine-year-olds to the scholarship boys. By my second term I was in full charge of boy boarders. The headmaster of the boys' day school was an Oxford man of forty with a Spanish wife and a belief, inculcated from the Misses Grey-Moffat, that I was twenty-seven years old instead of my actual eighteen. This deception was encouraged by the principals who took every advantage from it and put me to teaching the senior girls, some of whom were older than me. When I saw that I was to be used as a senior master on the initial pittance given to me, I objected and gave in the first of my resignations—done the simple way of bawling down the grand hallway at the elder Miss Grey-Moffat during one of the daily staff rows.

And yet Caroline College was one of the best schools I ever had dealings with. Somehow, large numbers of the children passed examinations. They did well at games and in fact were altogether fitted to rule and run an Empire which everybody seemed to have forgotten no longer existed. Most of the pupils showed no symptoms of having complexes or sexual difficulties. At the series of confirmations the candidates smiled as benignly at the bishop as he smiled at them. The Girl Guides were well-turned-out and the Boy Scouts were something to be proud of—which was more than they were of me. When my powers of organization received official recognition I was hurriedly shoved into a Scout-master's uniform and promptly put in charge of the school troop. Unfortunately, the sheep's clothing did not completely disguise the wolf for I disgraced the troop by attempting to shake hands with my right hand when the Chief Scout came to the county jamboree.

And then there was the St. George's Society—a curious affair full of patriotic mumbo-jumbo practised in affiliation with the London group of the same name. Even among the staff it was thought to be a privilege to belong. Not even the day boys' headmaster was acceptable, and apart from the Misses Grey-Moffat the only staff members in the society were Miss Nance-Trelawny and me. Both schools, however, were expected to attend such of St. George's affairs as were conducted in public. It was surprising how many Days and Birthdays connected with battles or royalty could be crowded into one term. At innumerable public meetings we were all under constant exhortation to stand up for, stick up for, or otherwise support and save from collapse an eclectic mixture of ideals, principles, and concrete objects such as the Union Jack, as well as abstract concepts such as the British Empire.

The society was well adapted to those whose pleasure in life was derived from being exclusive rather than in belonging to the crowd. The music master at Caroline College had not got sufficient votes to become a member of the St. George's Society and I thought it noble of him to produce music to order for various occasions, teaching his singing classes such stuff as:

Stand up for the old, old country,
Uphold its glory and its fame,
As our fathers did before us
They not only sang in chorus
But by deeds inspired us all to do the same.

He was a clever musician who was never interested in climbing the ladder of success. Perched a few rungs down from the top he was content to teach and turn out occasional compositions, nearly all of which he dedicated to the memory of his 'brave niece' Amy Johnson the flier.

My loathing for the St. George's Society was the main fly in the Caroline College oitment. Yet I had no alternative but to join. The society simply seemed to me yet another activity I must take up in order to practice the difficult art of 'getting on'. Getting on had become my life's sole ambition.

Most of the society's activities seemed to take place during my spare time and consisted of long-winded planning for the next public event, discussions as to whether threepence should be charged for watercress sandwiches if cucumber-and-cheese ones cost fourpence, since the proceeds were for stopping death-watch bettle in the church roof.

The members' meetings were held *in camera* in the kindergarten while the public functions took place in the banqueting hall. Here the Misses Grey-Moffat turned up in full evening dress regalia, the best parsnip wine was hauled up from the cellars and served to such celebrities as the vicar or the school dentist.

These do's for National Days in the banqueting hall were matched in enthusiasm only by those for Holy Days which centred round the parish church where we sat under the memorial window to the Founder of Caroline College, the Misses Grey-Moffat's mother. Magna Charta Day was a peak celebration when we all stood round the flag pole for an hour singing hearts-of-oak kind of songs followed by yet another public gathering in the school gymnasium when the significance of Magna Charta was explained to the audience who forgot it again immediately afterwards. St. George's Day itself, that Double of First Class of all Doubles, usually occurred during the vacation, though even then we were supposed to assemble in London for the laying of a wreath on the Cenotaph and a march to St. Paul's with roses in our buttonholes and praises in our hearts for belonging to the greatest nation on earth.

Inevitably, the links forged in the school formed themselves into a chain of contacts and activities outside the school. I was no longer always present to hear the women members of staff squabbling as to which of them should mend my socks. However, it was important that my socks should not have holes, because I entered a brief and inglorious career as an actor.

The same compulsion must have been driving me which previously made me want to preach. Acting in staff plays and producing others for parents' day at the school, whetted the dulled edge of my platform manner. An opportunity came to play a small part at Ilfracombe's Pavilion Theatre with a company doing a season there, and I accepted. The Misses Grey-Moffat had no objections since it would not interfere greatly with my teaching duties. They even brought several parties all the way to the theatre to see me perform.

The Irish Players from Dublin were at Ilfracombe's other theatre, and I became friendly with one actor who was also the company's stage manager. Paddy Coyle and I had met before,

But how different we both had been then. I was a scruffy Belfast evacuee suddenly flung into Fermanagh, and Paddy Coyle was a student visiting his family up the hill from the herdsmen with whom I was billeted. I thought it strange that Fermanagh should pursue me still, seven years after I used to see Paddy cycle by our cottage.

Later on, Paddy Coyle encouraged me to try and make a career in acting. But meanwhile I was still stuck like a limpet on the rock of Caroline College, only becoming detached during vacations when I shot off as quickly as possible to the Continent. I became blasé about crossing the English Channel. It never compared in terms of excitement with my first crossing of the Water between Ireland and England. And like first love, nothing was ever quite the same as that. But equipped by Mama with a whole range of new tastes and the manners to exploit them, braced by self-confidence induced by my success at Caroline College, for the first time in my life having a substantial lining to my pocket, I was ready to enjoy what the Continent had to offer. Paris became my Bute Street.

At half-term or during long week-ends I went up to London, or sometimes with a tent to the New Forest and sometimes to Glyndebourne. And very often too, I went to stay with a man who was one of my referees for Caroline College. Sir Otto Mundy's house, Winterfield, stood on a hill above the Thames at Cookham. And Otto's house was no museum of the Fine Arts, no repository for priceless Donatellos as was Evan Morgan's stately Tredegar Park. Winterfield was a lived-in house. Instead of statues and figurines, Otto Mundy's hall contained two enormous cylinders which supplied Otto and his guests with soda water for their whisky. The metal cylinders were typical of Otto's extravagantly generous attack on life. He never did anything by halves and in this resembled Evan Morgan. To hear the cylinders roaring like a jet engine into somebody's glass of whisky was to hear the music of Winterfield. And it played constantly for the many people who came and went.

One rainy winter night while the cylinders were roaring I went to the front door and found a most extraordinary and

Dandelions and the Rape

dirty-looking little man standing wet-through on the doorstep. The rain hung in beads on his tangled donkey-fringe. A far-away look, not unlike that of Myrtle Dailes's, occupied the eyes, as though the visitor had just lighted on us from another planet. He almost had, for this was Stanley Spencer. After our unworldly meeting at Otto's front door, I often used to come across the artist rambling in the country lanes round about Cookham or along the river.

By the invention of such phrases as Purchase Tax, Otto enlarged the English language, for his role as a high-ranking civil servant placed much responsibility in his hand. But his mind was not limited to matters of national finance. At Cookham he was a legendary host, especially to people connected with the arts. Otto's rotund figure rolled about helpless with laughter on the Thames's banks at Stanley Spencer's adventures with the old pram which held his painting gear. Yet with equal force Otto could be moved to tears. A. E. Housman's poetry always moistened his eyes, for Housman wrote some of his verse while staying at Winterfield.

Motoring gave Otto another thrill. At illegal and alarming speeds he loved to dash along the roads, perhaps to sample the food at a new restaurant. Or he would flee up to London where the Café Royal was a favourite meeting place. Or as I would be in a Somerset lane taking the boarders to some rugged north coast cove for swimming, there would be the roar of an engine, the squawk of brakes and a beaming Otto would get out, bringing with him an enormous basket of strawberries for the boys' picnic lunch.

Otto was not happy unless he was giving his friends presents. The best he ever gave me was to whisk me off to Glyndebourne. The beauty of the place astonished me and so did the music. The combination of the two went to my head and stayed there from that day on. And at this time Glyndebourne gave me friends who are still my friends and brought me my first contact with another stage manager, Patrick MacClellan. Later he embroiled me in some exciting theatrical adventures ranging from grand opera to the *Fol-de-Rols*.

Dandelions and the Rape

When we met, Patrick was on the Glyndebourne staff—a huge hulk of a man laughing and joking as he went through the moonlit Sussex lanes to find a pub. The young woman walking beside him and who shared his laughter intrigued me. I had heard her sing and admired her as a person. Kathleen Ferrier was on her way to the village with Patrick for what in her biography was called 'a dirty big pint'.

What a dazzling sun was shining on me now, in my nineteenth year, only seven years after I had left the shadows of my Belfast childhood for the last time. It was marvellous to know such a woman as Kathleen Ferrier. I discovered Benjamin Britten's bitter-sweet music which Kathleen had sung with another woman who became a lasting friend, Anna Pollak. When the curtain went up for *The Rape of Lucretia* it also rose on a time in my life dominated by music and music-makers as it had once been by religion and preachers. By coincidence, my involvement with music came to a close with Lucretia's untimely death.

When, some years later, Patrick MacClellan went off to Southern Rhodesia to supervise and direct the special theatre being built for the Rhodes Centenary Exhibition, I was the London agent. This linked me closely with all the excitement, for London's big companies, from the Old Vic to Covent Garden, were going out at one time or another during the celebrations. Among the hundreds of artists and musicians who flew out from London Airport, there was only one cancellation. Kathleen Ferrier could not go, as planned, to sing with the Hallé orchestra. When the plane loaded with members of the company had gone, I took some flowers to Kathleen from the Exhibition. Her wonderful smile lighted me into the room where she lay propped up in bed. Was there any truth, I wondered, in the rumours about the terrible nature of her illness?

But Kathleen seemed to be as full of vitality as ever. With the old enthusiasm she showed me a Victorian Easter egg given her by somebody at Covent Garden. Then we talked about friends we had in common in the business. Kathleen discussed her discovery of delight in painting and in her new garden. It was late when I left and as I was going out of the room Kathleen called me back and asked me to bring Anna Pollak on my next visit.

As I turned and looked towards the bed there was sadness in her lovely face. It was an expression which always haunted me afterwards. Shadows were flying across the sunny landscape. The same melancholy suddenly took hold of me as when coming through the river-meadows at Cookham, Otto Mundy had spoken Housman's despairing lines 'Into my heart an air that kills. From yon far country blows.'

After this none of us had long to wait. And I think that Kathleen knew even that afternoon that there would be no more meetings, no more 'dirty big pints', no more beaming smiles in crowded dressing-rooms.

> *Far from those happy fields of Orpheus' song*
> *We wait for music by the shore.*
>
> *Soon the wind, late from the sad sea*
> *Brushes the unplucked strings, and is gone.*

CHAPTER XI

Schools of Thought

❧❦❧

Mama was proud of my achievement at Caroline College. But her pride was doomed to a short life for it was too delicate a thing to survive in this rude world. The world, in fact, obtruded itself into Meron House through the letter-box. Well indeed might the front door be barred and bolted against the marauding Jesuit Gestapo, but keeping the mail out was impossible. And through the mail, Mama experienced her first disappointment in me.

After my first term at Caroline College, streams of letters followed me to Meron House. At least two came from Myrtle Dailes every day, and Miss Fairweather felt quite 'queer' every time she went to the door for the parcel post. There was no mistaking Myrtle's beautiful handwriting, nor the exotic drawings covering the envelopes or wrappings. *What*, the two old ladies asked silently with quizzical eyes, what *ever* would come in the post next?

When Myrtle was taken in a cruel and inhuman way to the asylum, fears grew at Meron House. The flood of Myrtle's letters dwindled to a trickle, and then almost dried up after she lost the use of her right arm in trying to escape. But it was the idea of her escaping which really upset Mama. Violet, her own daughter, ended up in a home, but she was gentle and docile, whereas Myrtle was wild, and also dangerous when her captors moved in to seize her.

Myrtle did break out of her prison once. She came straight to me, bearing a load of chrysanthemums in her arms. For the few hours we were together it was as though some bright seraph had alighted at my world. Myrtle trailed stars behind her and there were stars in her eyes. But the baseness of uncharitable, unfeeling society caught up with her and she was forced back behind walls. There had been a time when she would sit up the whole night covering sheet after sheet of paper with criticisms of my youthful poetry. The glitter and sadness of her blue eyes, as she thrust those woolly-headed chrysanthemums at me burned a mark in me which never afterwards faded.

But although Myrtle seldom wrote now, a large number of other letters plopped into the letter basket at Meron House. Mama was always uneasy. As I had spied on Miss Fairweather as she secretly curled her hair, so she now spied on me, reporting to Mama every time a new or unfamiliar post-mark appeared on my mail. Miss Fairweather always picked up the letters so that she was able to see the post-mark. This was a done thing, unlike the reading of postcards which was not done because it was 'common', a practice in which Aunt Mabel's working-housekeeper was strongly suspected of indulging.

Myrtle's letters, however, were not the only ones which Mama had cause to fear. There were Colette's also. I had met Colette through Myrtle. Colette's warm, generous nature had led her into worry and concern over her friend Myrtle, whose increasing detachment from mundane realities threatened to attract the unwelcome attentions of well-meaning authorities. I was immediately drawn to Colette. What could we do about Myrtle? The answer seemed to be nothing. Yet Colette sucked me into a vortex of responsibility for Myrtle and thereby, unintentionally, formed a bond between herself and me.

Colette was not without her own trouble. A cloud of unhappiness dulled the bright colours of her vivacious nature. In the end, I began to be more concerned about Colette than about Myrtle. Colette's husband Tim had returned from the war to accuse her of being the lover of a man who, by a curious coincidence, I also knew. Mama had originally introduced me to him rather proudly for he was her favourite politician and represented a seat which had formerly been part of her brother-in-law's constituency.

Poor Miss Fairweather liked to think that the politician, who lived in her home town, had smiled at her in a meaningful way during a garden party. Miss Fairweather insisted that this had been so and as a result Mama referred to him as Don Juan. Surprisingly, Mama had no objection for she was much impressed by him as public figure. Even on a Sunday Mama had turned the wireless on and we sat together listening to his broadcast.

Colette lived with Tim in a cottage balanced over the sea on the cliffs in Cornwall, and I often went to stay with them. Myrtle had an open invitation but by this time it had already become impossible for her to go anywhere. And although Colette genuinely regretted this, I saw that she wanted me to herself and this would have been impossible with Myrtle present. Without any conscious effort at intrigue, Colette wanted me around to act as a buffer between Don Juan and Tim.

Colette had got herself into a complicated emotional tangle. The other two men were too involved themselves to see or act clearly. And this was no simple case of infidelity or duplicity. Colette's unhappiness ran deep. At that juncture she badly needed a new confidant who could apply cold reasoning to the problem. So we walked along the moonlit Cornish beaches, talking avidly, and occasionally abandoning ourselves to the soporific sluicings of the sea and the softly bemusing light of the moon.

Nobody, least of all Colette and I, thought that anything more than innocence and sympathy promoted these shore walks. But I found myself looking forward to being alone with Colette. The sharp smell of the sea and the cries of gulls became inseparable in my mind from her presence. I ceased to care whether we found a solution for her dilemma, or whether we even so much as discussed it. It was wonderful just to be with her, especially since there, among the rocks and salty pools, she was more relaxed, more gay, more herself than in the rather taut atmosphere of the cottage.

I was infatuated with Colette. She filled my mind as the sun illumined the sky and irradiated the bland acres of the sea with glancing lights. Colette's problem remained, though now its geometry was more complex for the triangle had become a quadrangle. My principal motive was to save Colette from Don Juan. Not only was he already married but he was making a fool of the lovable Colette, who deserved better treatment.

Don Juan's own motives in pursuing her seemed to me to be excessively selfish. Colette's healthy youth appealed to his own patronizing middle-age. She was good-looking and temperamentally incapable of any kind of reserve. Don Juan played upon her good nature. Her husband, he said, had not been able to give her a child, so why should not he sire one himself? It would, Don Juan claimed, be a magnificent child. It would have Colette's own physical beauty and Don Juan's great intellect. He pestered poor Colette unmercifully. Yet she could not see that he did not love her as a whole person, but only as the projected image of his own desires.

My dislike of Don Juan was not entirely guileless, and male jealousy was involved. He resented Colette's playful antics with me along the beach and suffered agonies over our long rambles across the moors. Don Juan may have been a clever man, and though he lost no opportunity in letting other people know this, I did not think him so brilliant as our mutual friend Evan Morgan, many of whose interests he shared. It was only when *The Times* obituary of Don Juan claimed years later 'It is as a poet, critic and man of letters' that he would be remembered, I realized he had been interested in anything other than politics and parliamentary committees.

Apart from the vexed question of getting a child, I could not see what Colette found attractive about Don Juan. She made it clear, and here for once she took a decision, that she would never leave Tim, neither for Don Juan nor for me. We laughed about that, and abandoned our young bodies to the sea and the shore-winds. We swam and frolicked and when we thought nobody else was looking disported ourselves ridiculously. We stole kisses on the moors, and returning at night pranced a parody of the Cornish floral dance through the village streets.

Tim was strangely diffident. Yet he did not resent Colette spending her time with me. It was as though I made up for his own lack of confidence. We were friendly and often went out together with the local fishermen for conger eels. When we all went off to dances in parish halls Tim insisted I should dance with Colette for he disliked dancing and had never learned to do so.

Mama knew about this Cornish *ménage à trois*, for I told her all about it—or nearly all. Of course, she recoiled. Whenever Don Juan's name was mentioned in the papers or on the wireless she went white. Scandal was in the air, even on a national scale, and Mama wanted Meron House well clear if any trouble should break. Meanwhile, Colette's letters to me continued to arrive at Meron House. They were always long letters folded fatly into large envelopes and often carrying enclosures of Don Juan's love-letters or her husband's notes of love or accusation which Tim wrote in his worst moments of desperation. Each letter brought new terror to Mama and Miss Fairweather. They could see the policeman walking up the drive to make enquiries. Fortunately, Mama was dead before such dire depths were reached.

But the arrival of a parcel was my undoing. It made Mama adamant that I must leave Caroline College and go as far away from Cornwall as possible. Miss Fairweather brought the parcel into the drawing-room together with Mama's mid-morning celery juice, taken for her arthritis. I opened the parcel and there, before the two astonished ladies, lay two of my shirts sent on from the school's Somerset laundry, *and* (and this demanded the smelling salts), a pair of green bloomers belonging to the senior mistress.

Even when Miss Nance-Trelawny herself wrote to explain how the laundry had been delivered late and how her own missing garment had inadvertently got into my parcel, Mama was still unappeased. The world, she said, was getting 'queerer' every day. She herself had relatives whom she knew for a fact did not turn their mattresses from one week's end to another. But never had she expected to find a stranger's bloomers on her own drawing-room table.

This had a far more drastic effect on Mama than even a press cutting she saw about my theatrical activities. After all, she loved puppets and had liked Gilbert and Sullivan in her far-off, unsaved youth. But my precious soul *was* 'saved' already. I must therefore be protected. It was obvious that Caroline College was crammed full of unsaved women, all of whom were in the dangerous forties. Though I tried to please Mama over most things, I did not want to leave Somerset. The place appealed to me and I had grown used to its crazy ways. But Mama would not hear of it.

After what Mama called the 'nasty package' had arrived, I went off alone to Paris, where, amongst other and more physical business, I attended some of the goings-on at the Rue des Colonels Rénards. My ears were emptied of Miss Fairweather's clip-clopping along the cool passages of Meron House and filled with high-pitched voices of young men reading and the Russian-accent English of Gurdjieff's stuffy, overcrowded temple. Little did I know then that those weeks of eyes-closed contemplation (about what? I could never remember afterwards) around the master-magician himself wearing a fez, were going to disrupt everything I held dear in life.

Back in London again I spent a week-end with Paddy Coyle. On the first evening he asked if I would like an audition for a part in *Shadow and Substance*. With such a prospect I could not say no. In effect, I now agreed with Mama. My days at Caroline College were over. The week-end in London became four months. But I did not succeed in being an actor. Dreary rounds of agencies and Sunday night try-outs drained my enthusiasm and perhaps I was keener on the glamour than on the work and the long climb to success. It never occurred to me that perhaps, also, I had no talent for acting. Christmas came too soon again and I was glad to hear Mama's 'Are you there?' on the telephone with an entreaty to spend Christmas at Meron House. I went at once and relaxed as the tranquillity and comfort of the place enveloped me. It was my home.

As always, Mama had a scheme up her sleeve. Since, she said, I was happy in teaching why did I not beseech the Lord to lead me into a sound Christian school? And once again the Lord was positively pushed into fixing me up. As for Mama, once again no doubts existed in her mind that the Lord *was* leading me. Neither did similar doubts trouble the Reverend Headmaster of Fernville Preparatory School in Birmingham. On the very evening when he was telephoned about me, he was in the act of writing out an advertisement for *The Times*. He needed a mathematics master to take the senior boys working for public school scholarships. That I was 'saved' was the great thing, for even mathematics were apparently better if they were evangelical. Assured of my religious convictions it remained for the elder Miss Grey-Moffat to convince him that my mathematics were as good as my soul. Then everybody sat back comfortably and proclaimed, over yet one more coincidence, that the Lord was leading.

This time, however, the leading went a little astray. From the outset I was unhappy at Fernville. The prim dull Birmingham suburb was a poor exchange for the beautiful countryside around Caroline College. The screams of laughter and tears and the blood-boiling brawls of the Somerset staff-room had been heaven compared with the smug, emasculated atmosphere of the equivalent room at Fernville. The rose-hip gatherings on the moors became tours of chocolate factories. In my new school most of the staff were 'saved' and several were clergymen.

Although Fernville was Church of England by name, by inclinations it leaned towards strict Baptist. Nothing mattered so much as being 'saved'. Many of the boys had already 'come out on the Lord's side'. When I went into the senior dormitory while on my evening duty, I had to lead the boys in prayer. After I had finished, there had to be a silence for any boy to add his own *ad lib.* prayers. This usually meant that the 'saved' prigs would brag about their soul's condition at the expense of the 'unsaved'. But in spite of this intense social pressure many boys resisted manfully and left for their public schools as whole and healthy sinners.

If the dormitory prayers were embarrassing, the after-supper staff ones were even more so. Apart from anything else, it was bad for the digestion. These prayer-meetings were convened with the sole purpose of forcing the Lord's hand into saving the school housekeeper's soul. The Lord was given exactly one term to bring about this change of heart. Should He fail and let His faithful down, sterner measures would be taken. The housekeeper was a thorn in the flesh to the female teachers and when she still refused to raise her hand at a public meeting, many of the women staff resigned.

I liked the housekeeper and by this time was using her sitting-room in preference to the staff-room. The attraction was also due to the school matron, Margaret, who, as school matrons go, was young and not very matronly. She showed as few signs of being 'saved' as I did. We joined forces with the non-resident music mistress and physical training instructor and invaded as many old pubs around Warwickshire as we could find. We also spent some godless Sunday afternoons boating on the Avon while the school became headquarters for hundreds of chorus-singing Crusaders.

Our unholiness could not long go undetected, of course, and a watch committee was set up. It became unbearable even to have tea in the staff-room. The evangelical twitterings fell silent as I entered, and an anti-Catholic, anti-Irish campaign began. The chief protagonist in this was Mrs. Lowcock. She brought all her sixty years of life with Irish Catholics in Liverpool to bear on the eating of our corned-beef sandwiches.

Margaret was not always free to come for cream cakes in the High Street with me, so occasionally I faced the staff-room and Mrs. Lowcock. This good evangelical lady ranted on about Southern Ireland and Spain being backward and poverty-stricken because they were priest-ridden, just as Liverpool had its slums because the city was full of Irish Catholics. Mrs. Lowcock had an extensive repertoire of similar clichés which were as offensive as they were tedious.

Things clearly could not go on for I made it plain that I had more sympathy for the Catholic garbage of Liverpool's back streets than I had for the starched smugness of the Birmingham common room. Also, while moving about on the Continent I had picked up oddments of Baroque art. A worm-eaten Madonna and Child standing in my room did not improve relations. And at last the explosion came. I told Mrs. Lowcock what I thought of her and that she was the last person I should have thought qualified to say whether Liverpool's Catholics were heathen or not. I slammed the staff-room door and handed in my notice to the Reverend Headmaster.

For Margaret, this was an enormous joke. Together, we plotted to shock the staff as often as we could during the half a term which now remained to me. I began by going back to the school at night, pretending to be drunk and reeling about the drive. I also went openly to the theatre at Stratford-on-Avon with 'unsaved' parents of my pupils. When my scandalously late nights happened nearly every night and my nocturnal singing became louder and bawdier, Mrs. Lowcock grew afraid when I went up the stairs to the staff quarters. Then Margaret and I bought an engagement ring for a shilling in Woolworths. She wore it at breakfast next morning. But nobody congratulated us as we intended they should. Instead, the Reverend English Master got up and went to whisper the terrible news to the Headmaster's table. We kept the sham engagement going for the rest of the term.

The next move was a bigger bombshell. I was away one week-end at Cookham but returned early to the school in Otto Mundy's car. It was a baking Sunday and so I collected my swimming things and we went together down to the Avon. Before we left Margaret came flapping a letter for me, delivered while I was away. The headmaster of the preparatory department of Clayesmore in Dorset had written to accept me for the following term. I was so delighted that I flung my arms around Margaret in wild excitement. Unfortunately she was sitting on the edge of her bed. Stressed beyond normal with our combined weights the bed collasped with an almighty crash and an unseemly scream from Margaret. In the room beneath us the heads of young Crusaders bowed in prayer looked up in shock and amazement.

The Woolworth's engagement ring was only set with glass and I was not in love with Margaret any more than I was with Myrtle Dailes or Colette. But I had fallen in love with somebody who had Mama's approval. I knew Rosemary pleased the old lady, for Mama did something very queer indeed. She bought me a book which did not come out of a Bible colporteur's suitcase. The book was V. Sackville-West's *English Country Houses* and Rosemary's home appeared in it. Her father was a great landowner whose ancestral home was as famous for its architecture as for the works of art it contained. Even though it was only on the scale of Bournemouth and Farnham I had become quite used to living with wealthy people. Both Rosemary and her father had titles to go with the glories of house and estates, but the influence this exerted over an ex-cabin boy from Belfast's back streets was less than might have been expected. And since Rosemary and I spent our week-ends together in London, her relations and her august family background hardly entered our two lives at all.

At Clayesmore, I was earning less than half what Rosemary paid an agent for looking after her personal estate in Yorkshire. What did we care, either of us, for the niceties of our respective stations? We cared nothing, for we let ourselves be carried away by happiness like a punt drifting on a summer river. Rosemary was the first girl-friend with whom I had ever experienced a fullness, with whom I could be completely myself, especially the new self which had developed as a result of leaving Ireland.

Although Rosemary's seat was in Yorkshire and mine was in Dorset at Clayesmore, we made London our common stamping ground. I grew accustomed to scudding off to Salisbury for the London train at week-ends. Rosemary went frequently to Africa, and then I seemed to spend every free teaching period cycling into Blandford with closely-scribbled airmail letters. Rosemary added sweetness to security, and success and my life was complete. I settled down to enjoy Clayesmore, basking in the sun now risen over my life.

From the week-end when I went to Dorset for the interview and stayed at a cottage in the old village of Charlston Marshall, I knew things would go well. Clayesmore was an island in the beautiful Dorset landscape. The staff lived in cottages or converted out-buildings. One master kept a goat, another parrots. In my own cottage, once installed, I let loose a pandemonium of indoor plants which were always being knocked over when the boys of my house swarmed around the open cottage fire on winter nights.

But at Clayesmore winter passed as though it were no more than a cold snap between the last gold of autumn and the first green of spring. But there was never time to wonder whether January frosts, February mud, or March gales would last. Soon, it seemed, wild flowers covered the hills and lay thick about the newly-leafed woods again, and the softest of cloudshadows drifted across the parkland round the school. With shouts and splashings and the restless quick movement of young bodies the River Stour's deepest bends echoed to our swimmers. At evening, when bats fled out of the boathouse across to the river-island where the Scouts met, I took older boys up-river where their rivals at Bryanston lived. Although our boys were building a boat, we all preferred an ex-American rubber landing craft for these hilarious jaunts.

There were long cycle rides with hordes of muscle-bound boys which nearly always ended in collisions, not with cars for we never saw any along those lonely lanes, but with gory strawberry teas discovered in prim teashops. There were less prim pints in Charlston Marshall's cottage kitchen pub where the farm cider went to many heads as the handsome blond head of the school's chef, a Pole, went to many hearts.

There were other emotions which only art could relieve, so the art room and the potter's oven were busy. And there were physical feelings which only the sports field and cricket pitches could relieve. Horses were ridden under the trees in the park. Rugby was played in season with its striped shirts and surges of movement, but in the summer sunlight runners disappeared over the hills and went far away, white specks in a green landscape. There were puppets in the school's carpenter's shop and living actors on its stage, sometimes acting what I had written.

I never knew how much the contentment of that time was due to Clayesmore or how much was due to Rosemary. I was too happy and too busy to think of such things. When Rosemary was abroad I still dashed into Salisbury at week-ends for the London train. My insatiable curiosity was leading me deeper into the toils of so-called 'higher learning' and I was involved with a Gurdjieff group in London. How esoteric we were! How I stuffed my head full of ideas from the Master himself and from students and followers of his who once belonged to the Institute for the Harmonious Development of Man at Fontainebleau. Ouspensky and Orage were my apostles, though Katherine Mansfield was the only one whom I actually enjoyed. Next best thing to Gurdjieff's own Paris apartment on the Rue des Colonels Rénards was to join in with a London group. I was still at an adolescent stage when Groups and Clubs and Societies and Institutes and Associations seemed necessary to life.

My group had originally been part of Ouspensky's large circle. His very recent death left the circle without a centre and other circles were added to it like ripples in a pond. Many of the people dashed off to Paris again. But I went to Eaton Square in London. Not for me was the pickled yak from Tibet, the specially-flown peaches from the Azores, eaten in the company of starry-eyed Americans who washed the 'higher learning' down with vodka and rare liqueurs. While in Paris, it had not taken me long to see exactly how powerful most of the students' psyches were.

I had my wits about me and in spite of bogus devotees, I did not abandon the idea that 'higher learning' and 'eternal recurrence' contained something of value. Among the Beulah Bible Academy's students, David had been in himself sufficient reason for me to continue belief in God. Among the do-good but obnoxious women trying to 'save' the sinful world, Sister Edna alone was proof that doing good was not always a bad thing. Similarly, I hoped that amongst the Gurdjieff higher learners there might be some people at least who would justify the whole process. In the first instance I had been particularly interested in Gurdjieff's powers of healing. But I found better results in a Dorset mansion. This was run by the father of a Clayesmore pupil.

Gurdjieff's attraction was curious. Not only the novelty-seeking rich and the spiritually hypochondriac went to him, but many sincere intellectuals and scientists and doctors. And there were clergymen whose faith had worn threadbare. When I met Martin I thought he was one of these. I did not know whether he was first drawn to the Ouspensky circle because of the course in medicine he had done as a young man or because of his interest in comparative religion. Martin appeared to me as a quiet, gentle old Church of England clergyman. The invitation to visit his group in Eaton Square seemed as innocent as his own round face and guileless eyes.

I went and found him in a library that was mellow and mature with its floor-to-ceiling lining of books, which allowed only space enough for windows, a painting by Constable and an unidentified picture of John the Baptist over the fireplace. Books were littered about the other rooms also. Those which could not be organized into bookcases were stacked on floors, overflowing into the hallway and the bathroom. Martin and I already had common ground to work on for he had been at Radley and later at Oxford with Otto Mundy.

I had no inkling of what was to follow my call at the house in Eaton Square. In his novel *Strange life of Ivan Osokin*, Ouspensky showed how a magician prophesied that should Osokin live his life over again, he would also make the same mistakes once again. But should ever my life come to me again, certainly I would never go again so willingly to my own destruction as I did on that day. Nor would I go again down the corridor into the library where the maid showed me in to the old man who sat smoking a pipe. The dear old clergyman was leprous with evil.

It took me some time to discover Martin's obsession with evil. Meanwhile my youth and curiosity and a name I had earned myself in the group for being a faith healer, were my contribution to this new acquaintance. The healing business was much simpler than the group members either would or wanted to believe.

I was sure that the roots and herbs which the tinkers on Belfast's Bog Meadows gave me when I was a child were far more effective against my various childish ailments than the emulsions and malts provided by the municipal authorities at the tuberculosis clinic, if only for the plain reason that as often as possible I avoided taking the emulsions and malts but swallowed the tinkers' herbs in vast quantities.

When I was an evacuee in Fermanagh, I saw for myself that the soft mucilage of common wayside mallow was much more beneficial to the ills of horses than the expensive visits from the vet. Also, love potions and herbal teas excited me, though for a long time I resisted charms for sickness and broken bones. I distrusted these charms, inherited usually by word of mouth at some charmer's death-bed, because poor Maggie once wore an amulet of wool for a broken arm, until the pain and the inflammation grew unbearable and she went off to the hospital in Enniskillen. Something of this conviction that there is more in medicine than mere medicines followed me in my 'saved' days when I went to many faith healing services. Armed with such country lore and city experience in faith healing mission-halls, I impressed (not to say hoodwinked) the Eaton Square group.

Martin was convinced I had 'the gift'. He swore that I had cured at least one of his many ailments. And indeed perhaps I did. But since most of his disorders were caused by lack of exercise, over-eating, over-drinking, and over-indulgence in many things less innocent than either eating or drinking, effecting a cure was neither miraculous nor difficult. Martin had always been cursed with ample independent means and since coming down from Oxford had never been obliged to work.

Nevertheless, to satiate yet another of his desires, that of religious experience, Frank took Holy Orders and was actually a curate for a few years at St. John's Wood.

Martin enjoyed the role of being the white sheep of his family. When several of his brothers, all as wealthy as himself, decided on ordination, Martin was furious. He took off his clerical clothes and never wore them again. At least, seldom wore them again. I saw him only once in black and with a dog-collar and that was for a livery dinner at the Fishmongers' Society. At home, however, in the leather-bound seclusion of his library or in the curtained drawing-room Martin dressed in his full priestly regalia to perform ceremonies which certainly could not be found in Krafft-Ebing.

After his curate days, Frank married and settled down with his children at Morecombe Manor near Bath. He went on a series of world travels hoping to find the secrets of esoteric learning. Unlike Gurdjieff, however, Martin was far too fond of this world's comforts and he found it difficult to compete with the Master in Mecca and Lhasa. Twenty weeks, let alone twenty years in Tibet would have killed Martin. All he learnt from travelling was that he could give himself bigger thrills and excitements at home, so when his sons married he returned to London where he set up house, outdoing the Rue des Colonels Rénards by its hospitality. Gurdjieff's apartment was the reward for years of hardship in the East and the entertainment was based on the rare and the exotic. But the table at Eaton Square surpassed that of the Rue des Colonels Rénards. Martin boasted that his cook was the best in England. As far as I could tell then, and as far as I have experienced since, he was right. She was a virtuoso playing to a sophisticated audience. The whisky and brandy sessions which followed dinner, however, were less sophisticated.

Somehow, perhaps out of reverence for food, Martin managed to stay within the bounds of propriety during dinner, for it was the most solemn hour in his day. It began with a Hebrew grace, and finished with a reading from the Penta-teuch by me. While grace was being said, it was proper to eat a corner of brown bread. And should Martin be sober enough, he would kiss the ground in humility, as an amen to the grace. This done, he sat down to what must have been one of the last remaining stately tables in Belgravia.

The meal proceeded with the extravagance of a gala performance. Grace was the overture and with the curtain up, course followed course like the scenes of an opera. But the programme was never repeated, to praise a dish meant that it would never be served again, for Martin prided himself on endless invention. To avoid the vulgarity of boring by repetition, the menu arrived by post a few days before the meal so that Martin could know any objection I might have and pass them on to his cook.

Martin had already decided to make me his protégé and doubtless felt embarrassed by my ignorance about food. Unknown to myself he was schooling me to occupy an important place in a wild project already in his mind at this time. Besides the arts of eating, Martin wanted me to learn those of drinking too and he opened the world's vineyards to me. When the menus arrived they read like poems. Years later he sent me one which was typical of the many during the early days,

Amontillado	Consommé Pompadour
Zeltinger Himmelreich Spätlese 1949	Truite Saumonée à la Gelée
Ch. Beychevelle 1934 Irroy 1943	Terrine de Perdreaux
Tuke Holdsworth 1922	Soufflé aux Cerises
Grande Champagne	Manx Toast

The splendour of the dining-room dazzled the eyes just as the meal seduced the palate. Its glitter, its sparkle and glow, the radiance of its many lights, the warmth of reflections from polished wood, filled me with new wonder each time I saw it. Candles blazed like masses of wild daffodils, turning the ancient oak table to a glistening lake on which sailed silver sconces and Waterford finger-bowls like crystal boats, where ranks of silver at each place lay like exotic fishes lurking in an

oriental pool, where claret and burgundy flashed like precious
stones and old malmsies burned in the candlelight like beeches
soaked in October sunshine.

Martin's dinners were timed to perfection. An electric bell-
push was concealed at his end of the table, by which he sent
messages to the kitchen about our progress. The servant
coming along the corridor with the cheese soufflé had to hurry.
As the dining-room door opened, Martin had to hear the
greaseproof paper being taken off, and see the crust rising
when the dish was brought in.

Night was essential to Martin's dinners. Nobody who saw
the dining-room by day could believe the drab room to be the
same. For cheerlessness it matched Mama's dining-room at
Meron House. Daylight revealed horsehair spilling out of the
armchairs, and showed mildew spots on the hunting prints,
and flakes of paint ready to fall from the ceiling. And the
Georgian chalices which had toasted so mysteriously during
the meal looked like tin cans on a sideboard heavy with silver
Victorian dishes and half-empty bottles. Martin knew that his
dining-room was a morgue by day, and so he never gave
luncheon parties. Darkness was his friend. He was a host of
twilight.

Yet the atmosphere of these dinners was sinister despite the
brilliance. The more I saw Martin and the more I began to
discover the diabolic workings of his mind, the more fascinated
I became. Martin loved to tell the Russian story of the rabbit
and the snake. It was soon clear to me that if I allowed Martin
to go on hypnotizing me with the fascination of his house and
all that happened in it, he would ultimately be my ruin. He
well understood that he was the snake and that I was the rabbit
who knowingly approached his doom. Many times I determined never to enter the Eaton Square house again. But I
always did, until the day came when the snake struck.

Although food and drink differed so widely between Eaton
Square and the Rue des Colonels Rénards, the actual meetings
for 'higher learning' were similar. Long and dreary readings
from Gurdjieff's own writings were intended to be illuminated

by Martin's own interpretation of the esoteric. But whereas it was usually young Englishmen who did the readings in Paris, it was nearly always French students who did ours.

Yet nothing could dislodge my older beliefs. Although the idea of 'eternal recurrence' had a certain appeal, I stopped short of committing myself more deeply to the group. Martin knew this. He never asked me to read aloud from *Tertium Organum* at dinner but from the Pentateuch. And as for *A New Model of the Universe*, I thought it feeble and lacking in humanity compared with the New Testament.

The meetings took place in the drawing-room since the library was kept away from circle affairs. When I went alone to see Martin, however, we usually sat in the big library. Among the hundreds of books most were connected with Jewish matters, and not a few of these dealt with cabbalism.

The other members of our circle all had Jewish-looking features and I discovered later were in fact Jewish, or as Martin liked to think, came from lapsed families. He would have taken his cook's masterpieces for granted had they not been the work of a woman previously in the service of a Jewish peer.

His interest in me apart from faith healing, was partly roused by my beak nose. He was convinced it showed I had Jewish blood, though I liked to think, more probably, that it came from the Semitic features of gypsies. Martin's preoccupation with me was flattering, however, and I did not care by what means I stole the limelight from the supercilious young Frenchmen who were better versed in 'the work' than I was.

But I scored over them principally with my supposed gift for healing which caught Martin's enthusiasm—particularly after a visit to Sussex, Martin's native county. He liked to spend the summer months there by the sea so that he could swim and go for long country walks. The walks took a variety of routes but the way home always brought us to one particular spot. Behind the gates stood an hotel building. But it had once been Martin's old home. He hated the place and the people in it. And it was by those gates that I first realized that Martin's mind was a labyrinth of dark caves, the lairs of hatred and fear and evil thoughts. His interest in me was only partly connected with the Gurdjieff group. It was a mere cover for his deeper purposes. Since I possessed the gift of healing, he reasoned within himself, was it not equally possible that I could use the gift for cursing also.

It was a humid August afternoon. Purple thunderclouds pressed low over the Weald and a sudden silence seemed to press down on us as we stood by the gates. With scarcely-suppressed malice, Martin urged me to curse the hotel and its occupants. He wanted me to curse it verbally and also to desecrate the place in less abstract ways. The rain began to lash down as we stood there and we dashed for shelter to the wall enclosing the grounds. I was frightened. In spite of the afternoon's oppressive heat, I began to shiver.

A hot bath and a drink at home helped me to recover from the incident. I thought it better forgotten, though it was the eeriest encounter I ever had. It was more uncanny even than being with Evan Morgan when he dressed in the clothes of the famous Welsh witch who had been burnt at the stake near his estate. By dinner time Martin's benign charm and humour had returned to conceal any sign of the afternoon's experience. Yet, although he had now come into the open and made it plain that he thought he could use me as a witch to curse whatever displeased him, Martin showed no regret or shame. He continually harped upon the fact that I was possessed of supernatural powers, and he was always telling other people about an incident on another of our Sussex walks. To me, it had been no more than what I had done many times when I was a boy in Fermanagh, but Martin saw it as witchcraft.

While walking towards the end of an afternoon we came to a stretch of road blocked by parked horse-trailers. There had been a gymkhana and the owners were taking their animals home. But one woman could not persuade her horse to go up the ramp into the trailer. Other people tried, by blindfolding the horse or enticing it with carrots and lumps of sugar. The horse had already kicked one ramp to pieces in an attempt to make it go in backwards. It seemed so easy to me. When I asked the crowd of young hunters and red-faced colonels to let me handle the horse they looked affronted. But after speaking softly to the horse for a few moments I led it into the box.

Handling a horse was just one of the things I first learnt from the tinkers on Belfast's Bog Meadows. For Martin, however, it was another demonstration of my supposed extraordinary powers, a knowledge of lore handed down from the House of David itself. Indeed, from that day on, in Martin's eyes, the only crime I could commit was to be late for dinner.

Martin found it a strain to think and behave other than as if the world and everybody in it were created for his own special benefit. Jealousy and possessiveness were his constant companions. He had the egoist's idea that anything he did or said was vitally interesting to others. And if events in the outside world did not correspond to his inner vision of them, he would not hesitate to alter their course. Deceived by his flabby, over-fed body and his mild eye into thinking him innocuous, people failed to see the ruthless man beneath.

Martin fawned upon me in subtle ways. He heaped attentions on me. I sensed that this was not for my sake but for his own. Perhaps he understood that his flattery fed my own self-importance and that he could hold me in this way. But he had to have another figure in his landscape to act as counterpoint to his own existence. Nevertheless, unconsciously, I resisted his unwanted and gradual incursion into my emotions and feelings. But Martin was determined that I should be at the receiving end of some of his more maudlin sentiments. One day by the sea in Sussex, I cut my foot badly on some broken glass. Martin was at once all attention and sympathy. It was only afterwards that I learnt he had scattered the broken glass himself on the beach because I was spending too much time swimming with my young friends and not enough with him.

Excessive in most things, Martin was no less so in his attempts to dominate and devour other people's lives. His labyrinthine mind was always engaged in some scheme, of which the broken glass was a comparatively mild example, to force people into being dependent on him. The snake never lacked for rabbits.

Martin was far from done with me. My foot healed, so threatening to take me out of the sphere of dependence on him. He was at no loss. Shortly afterwards the postcards began to arrive for me at Clayesmore. They were seaside postcards with unseemly messages scribbled on the back. I guessed that someone in the Eaton Square circle was sending them, but did not then suspect Martin's influence. The cards were sent in fact by someone else at Martin's instigation. And this was the first time I understood that forces I could not fight were closing round me, forces which were to destroy much of what I loved.

I was lost and bewildered, rended by opposing loyalties, devoured by remorse and regret. Whether I would or no, the Christian faith clung about me like an old coat. Nobody's life was as good as Christ's. Meron House was as difficult to escape from as Eaton Square. Getting married seemed to be the only solution, with a home of my own whose front door could be shut against wind and rain. Yet when I thought of myself as quietly domesticated, I knew that a wilder part of me never would be caged. Martin thought he had snared me in his tangled wood. Mama thought my feet were firmly set on the pilgrim way, stumble though I might from time to time.

When school duties allowed, I went to lie under the great trees in Clayesmore's park. The masses of leaves above me, heaving in the gentle summer winds like a sea swell, held no answers. I peered into books for wisdom but found none. Expecting help, I poured my tortured thoughts on to paper:

They said I should walk at the shadowed edge of the trees,
Not venturing to the yellow fields where hot bodies go,
Laughing and tumbling from first eye-bright sun to star-rise and cool breeze
Nor follow paths through thick flowers to rush-bank and river flow.
'Stay,' they said, 'here are last year's leaves trodden underfoot, where the secret mole creeps,
Run not into the burning light but stay and learn the sleep that ends all sleeps.'

Schools of Thought

I ran then to the knotted, cruel heart of the wood, their angry shouts
    behind,
'He is mad. Let the hidden tree-arm trip him. He will break bones,
    the young must learn by pain.'
Winter wood and dark, beyond the yellow fields, bind fast, hold,
    make blind,
And let your tortured limbs screech in the wind, louder than laughter
    I have heard and never will again.
Then came light, night shattering flames of love, and a strong hand
    'Come with us, this is the way
Wanderer in the forest, green-shower spring waits only for the day.'

CHAPTER XII

Fair Weather and Foul

❧❧❧

On top of the landing cupboard at Meron House, near the coil of fire escape rope, was a microscope and a collection of slides. They had once been part of the medical equipment used by Mama's doctor daughter as a student. And now they were being sent off to Clayesmore for use by the biology master. Mama was so delighted at my success in getting the job at Clayesmore, she responded in her usual way by wanting to give. She had also been pleased when the headmaster telephoned before I went to the school to ask if I could teach Scripture. The prospect of my giving countless boys the essentials of the Bible and the evangelical faith seemed such a good thing to Mama. She saw no reason why they should not also have the mice tongues and flies eyes of her daughter's slides. It cost her a lot to part with the microscope. Mama had treasured it for many years as her favourite child's possession.

Christmas came again and I went home once more to Meron House where a bigger welcome than ever awaited me. The dust-sheets were taken from my room days before my arrival. Hot-water bottles had been lovingly carried upstairs to the bed by Miss Fairweather. The enormous white counterpane crotcheted by the Curry ladies for Mama's trousseau was carefully draped over the bed. The windows were thrown open to clear the smell of lavender which had been drying on the floor. The dried seeds were for a London mission which put them into sachets with Biblical quotations for free distribution in hospitals. When all was ready, the two ladies held private prayer in my room, that it might be hallowed during my stay. Then they went downstairs to await my kisses.

Things looked set fair for a quiet but happy Christmas. It was spoilt by Miss Fairweather's snobbery. Mama called this failing of the lady-housekeeper her 'Heirs and Graces'. From her youth, when she was a governess, Miss Fairweather had been saving money. By the time I knew her, she had a few thousands, for besides her own savings several nest-eggs had come her way and, of course, she had expectations in Mama's will. And now, when I arrived from Dorset for the Christmas holidays, Miss Fairweather drew me aside to say that the Lord was at work. She felt most strongly moved to make me the heir of what little she had.

What lay behind this, I discovered, was not the Lord above but the death of a certain lord in East Anglia—Rosemary's father. He left no sons to succeed him, though two of his titles went to the female line. These ancient baronies had come through Rosemary's remarkable grandmother who was described in the book of the peerage as 'the eldest co-heir of the two great generals, the Duke of Schomberg and the Duke of Marlborough'. And this phrase was one we all soon knew by heart for Miss Fairweather had a mania for the peerage. Locked up with the secret oranges and curling tongs in her bedroom was an old copy of Burke. And now that there was talk of an engagement between Rosemary and me, Mama suspected Miss Fairweather of consulting Burke more enthusiastically than her *Daily Bread* notes.

Rosemary had first told me in the most offhand fashion about the titles which her father's death had brought her, during an interval in the theatre one evening. But with growing leanings towards socialism and the hope that one day we would have children of our own, I did not want her to use the titles. Rosemary never did use them though they remain unavoidably hers by right. Neither of us cared to be prisoners of the past. My Ulster ancestors had doubtless crossed to England as harvest labourers. Doubtless they wandered the English roads with sticks over their shoulders and bundles on the ends done up in blue handkerchiefs. Rosemary's forbears had strutted around Windsor with the blue garter. But what did we care for them or for the yawning social gulf between them? We sucked the sweet juice of our hours together until the present day was dry. Past or future were unreal as we lost ourselves in a play, or sat chatting in a quiet corner of the Ladies' Carlton Club or wandered on bright Sunday mornings in Regent's Park.

Rosemary and I wanted to forget the encroachment of society and position which could threaten our happiness. But Miss Fairweather had other ideas. She seemed determined to harp on just that aspect of my relationship with Rosemary which caused us some distress. At first, I tried to bear with it for Miss Fairweather was fond of me and had written unfailingly to me once a week ever since I first went away to teach in Somerset, as Mama did.

But the lady-housekeeper's endless chatter began to play on my nerves. With her Victorian governess, companion, lady-housekeeper's outlook, Miss Fairweather could not see things in my way. In her best governess accent she would recite the list of Rosemary's famous ancestors, John of Gaunt, Governors of Calais, Admirals of England, the illustrious name on the Letter of the Barons to the Pope in 1301. Miss Fairweather ground on and on relentlessly even after Mama summoned her into the drawing-room to explain how much it upset me.

But the lady-housekeeper's hobby had taken full possession of her. Despite every discouragement she still produced bits of paper covered with family trees noted on her days-off in the reference library from bigger and more up-to-date books of the peerage. We knew Miss Fairweather went there because she once left her reading glasses behind and could not see to peel the onions next day.

For the first part of the Christmas holiday, however, everything went well. Miss Fairweather brought in Rosemary's letters with the African stamps which I always had to give her. And although the lady-housekeeper did not really collect stamps she carried those from Rosemary's letters about as though they were sacred relics.

On Christmas Eve I offered to ice the cake because poor Miss Fairweather was behind with the preparations and steadily becoming more harrassed. I set to work in the kitchen stirring and mixing and squeezing white and pink icing, absorbed in my task. Miss Fairweather buzzed about and instead of doing her own work got in my way and blocked the light, talking all the time about Rosemary's lineage. When she fetched the secret Burke downstairs to prove a point, I could stand it no longer. It was Christmas Eve. When the cake was done I wanted to have a couple of hours in Bute Town. Miss Fairweather pushed Burke under my nose. Without hesitation, I put the icing nozzle down and picked up Miss Fairweather, Burke and all, and placed her on the high shelf over the fireplace.

Next to Jesuits, bulls and earwigs, the lady-housekeeper was most frightened of heights. A terror out of all proportion to her situation seized Miss Fairweather and she began to scream, long, loud, penetrating screams. I continued with the icing but Mama appeared, expecting perhaps to find Miss Fairweather being burnt alive. But seeing the tiny creature sitting exactly like a bird on a perch, Mama began to laugh.

I finished the icing, helped Miss Fairweather down from her shelf and went into Cardiff. When I got home later, however, Mama's amusement at Miss Fairweather's plight had vanished. While I was doing the rounds on Bute Street Mama had been working out how I must have lifted Miss Fairweather. And Mama had come to the conclusion that I must have touched the lady-housekeeper's elastic-stockinged, seventy-year-old legs, which was very improper. Moreover, Miss Fairweather was feeling decidedly 'queer' as a result of the experiment and might well have to take Christmas Day off.

Quite firmly, Mama said that I was never again to go into the kitchen, nor any other part of the house ruled by Miss Fairweather. The situation, I thought, was absurd. But perhaps the wonder was that the old ladies and myself, their age and infirmity with my youth and high spirits, had got on well together for so long. At any rate, the decline leading to my ultimate fall from favour, could be dated from that Christmas Eve and the icing of the cake. And from then on, Miss Fairweather became subject to 'queer' turns more often, turns which stayed longer at each visitation, until the day came when one of the turns carried her off altogether.

Back once more at Clayesmore I had a score of things to think about and Christmas at Meron House diminished in importance. But then the Easter vacation came, bringing not only a reluctance to spend time in Wales, but also my twenty-first birthday. In response to an invitation I agreed to go to Ireland with Otto Mundy who was bound on an official visit in the *Vigilant*, the flag-ship of the Chairman of Customs and Excise. On the eve of departure Mama telephoned and asked me to go home immediately. There were important matters to be discussed now that I had reached man's estate.

The first thing concerned 'the dear old Vicar'. This was Mama's name for Martin, with whom a mutual tie had developed. Many threads went to make this tie, not the least of which was their common admiration for the Jews. Missions to the Jews received as much attention from Meron House as did the Egypt General Mission. Indeed, Mama's concern with the salvation of Israel was so strong that she made one great personal sacrifice for the work. She gave up her chiropodist. Mama had been going to the same man for many years. In no small measure, his skill had kept Mama on her feet despite the crippling arthritis. But now an immigrant Jewish family had moved into the flats next door to Meron House. The Lord made it plain to Mama, that she must sink her selfish feelings on the matter, and transfer her patronage to the Jewish family, one of whose women was trying to establish a practice in chiropody.

Dismay struck Miss Fairweather. Monday visits to the chiropodist shed a light over her week. The long drive into Cardiff to see the dear little man was an excitement in itself, following as it did the easy morning's work of preparing the cold luncheon. Now this pleasure was swept away. The young Jewess was in Meron House itself on Monday morning to do Mama's feet while she still lay on the ottoman waiting for the elastic stocking stage of getting up. Tracts had been sent from London specially explaining for Jews the way of salvation and Christ's fulfilment of the Old Testament. Mama had a new toy to play with and she wrote to 'the dear old Vicar' about it.

Martin, in fact, was not nearly so old as he liked to pretend. The Master in Paris was supposed to be more than a century old, whereas he was only over seventy. Martin copied Gurdjieff in this absurdity as in others. Nevertheless, Mama was impressed as Martin intended she should be, and he played on another theme of common interest with Mama. This was centred on Bath. Martin never got over the loss of Morecombe Manor and still talked of trying to get a similar property in Somerset. Bath was a great love of Mama's, a love which she shared only with Paris—and Keswick because of its big tent convention with Bishop Taylor Smith.

When Mama returned to England from being 'finished' in Paris, she had been unhappy at home and was glad to stay with Aunt Gale in Bath, even though Aunt Gale was stone deaf and had no more than a hundred pounds pin money in the year. But there had been so many nice houses in and around Bath where Mama went visiting and played pianos in high-ceilinged drawing-rooms or sang the French songs she had so lately learnt from her music master in Paris. One of the houses whose gracious doors stood wide for the young girl was Morecombe Manor, which Martin had bought in later years.

Of all the threads which connected Martin and Mama, I was the strongest. Mama was delighted therefore when 'the dear old Vicar' suggested to her that I ought to enter the ministry of the Church of England. And remembering all those happy Lake District conventions with Bishop Taylor Smith, Mama wrote to the Bible Churchman's Missionary Society in Bristol, an evangelical college which her husband's family had amply supported over many years. I even spent a week there both looking over the place and being looked over. Martin did not approve. For him low church was as bad or worse than Roman Catholicism. He thought I should go to his own old college at Oxford. But ultimately nothing came of this either for Martin had already made up his mind in other directions. I was a healer, he reasoned, and therefore already a leader. I was not to be taught but to teach.

One of the people who remained faithful with Martin to the end in his Gurdjieff ideals was the man who had helped Ouspensky financially when he was setting up the centre at Virginia Water. Martin was not sure whether he would still be alive himself if I went forward for ordination and obtained a country living where he could come and take services. But, he argued, he *was* alive at that moment when my future was being weighed in the balance once more. He was also wealthy enough to indulge his fancy and set me up in another kind of church. He would instal me in a healing centre. It was, in fact, Martin's way of getting himself a tax-free country house again.

Mama was not told at once of this new plan. In her innocence of Martin's scheming and deceit, she still fondly imagined that I might leave Clayesmore and follow Bishop Taylor Smith, and the great Dean Lefroy of Norwich with his Bible Classes and Nave Services, to evangelical fame. But suspicions about Martin gradually infiltrated into Meron House and at last the bond between Mama and 'the dear old Vicar' began to show signs of snapping. Mama began to see that perhaps the old clergyman was not so 'dear' after all. And Miss Fairweather messing about as always in books of the peerage discovered evidence of a distinctly less pleasant side to Martin's life, a less assuring entry than that in *Crockford's*. He was divorced.

Worse was to follow, a nasty reminder of 'the Oscar Wilde trouble'. Martin had been fascinated on occasions to hear the stories of Mama's Cornish childhood, and about the vicar of Boyton and his daughter Minnie. And now Martin sent Mama a book by Minnie's infamous brother-in-law, who had been a frequent visitor to Morecombe Manor. Meron House was outraged when the book arrived. That poor, dear Minnie Walters had been mixed up in 'the Oscar Wilde trouble' was bad enough. But that Martin should be proud of his friend Alfred Douglas, was quite unforgiveable in Mama's eyes. When Miss Nance-Trelawney's bloomers had appeared inadvertently on the drawing-room table at Meron House, Mama had thought the ultimate in horrors had been reached. But when the nasty book inscribed to Martin by the wicked little lord, came in the post, Mama knew that her association with the once 'dear old Vicar' was ended. In less than an hour the book was out of the house again. Miss Fairweather felt quite 'queer' carrying the dreadful thing back to the post office.

Mama did not make a scene or write to Martin. She simply withheld her friendship. Although he wondered at the silence of Meron House, Martin did not guess at Mama's displeasure. Consequently, when the Easter holidays brought my twenty-first birthday, Martin's gift for me arrived at Meron House.

On opening the package I found a small whistle made of gold and mounted with jewels. It had once belonged to Percy Bysshe Shelley, passing down to Martin's wife who came from the poet's family. There was also an antique candelabrum. It had eight branches, but the little one intended for use by the servant could be taken off, leaving seven branches, so making the thing Jewish. But Mama had no eyes for the old silver work, but only for the dedicatory poem enclosed with the presents:

> *These little gifts to mark the fleeting hours*
> *Of one short year, you know how short it seems,*
> *The mystic wonder of spring's youthful flowers,*
> *The sunsets shared, the mutual fireside dreams.*
>
> *Though on the altar-stone of time and place*
> *These memories lie slain, self-sacrificed,*
> *Remember one who sometimes in your face*
> *Has seen a shadow as of the face of Christ.*

The tie was snapped at last. Mama had not many weeks to wait before restraint became open disapproval, with lawyer's letters in the offing. But Martin remained unaware of what lay

behind the silence at Meron House. He wrote to Mama saying
that he was devoting a portion of his capital towards setting up
a house of study. His intention was to imitate Gurdjieff's
centre at Fontainebleau. He was to be the teacher and I was to
be a healer. His mistake was in the way he approached Mama
regarding me. The house, he wrote in his letter, must be big
enough and worthy enough of 'the prophet'—meaning me.

All Mama's religious senses recoiled. Something was going
on which lay beyond her comprehension. Not only was it un-
healthy but, she suspected, ungodly also. Idolatry and priest-
hood in Roman Catholicism were bad enough. But that
Martin wanted to set me up as a kind of pagan prophet, horrified Mama—at first into sorrowful silence and then into outraged remonstration with me. She could not understand how
on the one hand I could 'break bread' with her and on the other
mix myself up with a lot of 'queer' people dabbling in matters
expressly forbidden in the Bible by God. She thought of Mad
John Martin's great works on the staircase—*The Fall of
Babylon, The Destruction of Sodom and Gomorrah, The Last
Judgement*. But those visions were nothing compared with the
evil things come on them now, in the midst of their very lives.

Mama's hurt lasted longer than her horror. She had lavished
on me the love she would have spent on grandchildren, and
now she felt her feelings betrayed. Through all the vicissitudes
of our relationship, I do not think Mama ever ceased to love
me, though she frequently had cause to disapprove of my
doings. Yet the fact that she had no grandchildren returned
with fresh strength to torment her. It seemed that only the
wicked flourished. Aunt Mabel's working-housekeeper had
just got two more grandchildren—two more birthdays and
Christmas presents to be taken every year out of the family
fortune. Such things were hard to bear, though the gathering
clouds of such wrongs could only be the sign of Christ's coming again, which surely could not be delayed much longer.

I went back to Clayesmore. The term got into swing. Dorset
was drowned in the green waves of summer. The world had
never seemed more voluptuous. But I was forgetting moments

that *had* been more voluptuous. The Meron House letter-box opened again one morning and yet another letter for me dropped into the basket.

When Miss Fairweather put it on Mama's tray she knew it was no circular. A post-mark that had once been familiar had appeared again—a Cornish one. Mama had successfully broken me away from Colette. She thought the affair was over. Colette and I had not exchanged correspondence for over a year. During this time I had become totally preoccupied with Rosemary and with making plans for the future. Thoughts of Colette did sometimes cross my mind and I imagined her and Tim settled down to amicable reconciliation in their cottage by the sea.

Mama prayed over the letter that morning. But misgivings assailed her. So many postcards and letters about me had arrived, most of which she classed as 'queer'. Mama pressed Miss Fairweather into service and the lady-housekeeper took up operational-station at the telephone while the lines to Clayesmore buzzed for me. My last letter to Colette, a refusal of a Christmas party at the cottage, had been worded by Mama herself. Now she was distraught that her attempts to extricate me from a delicate situation appeared to have been in vain.

At Clayesmore I answered the summons to the phone and was surprised to hear Mama's news. I asked her to read the letter out. Instead of Colette's usual enclosures—Tim's outrageous letters of abuse to Don Juan and the violently worded notes from the House of Commons in reply—out came a set of photographs of Colette. But the snaps showed a new Colette, a Colette radiant with the glow of her much longed-for motherhood. There was not the slightest shadow of doubt but that the little boy in the photographs was mine.

Confusion and pride set about me. At least Colette's great longings had been fulfilled. The only unfortunate aspect of this new situation was that Tim thought the child was Don Juan's, the man who had harped so much on the subject of siring a child by Colette, a child in which brains and beauty would be uniquely combined. Nevertheless, Tim accepted the boy for he loved Colette and was happy that she was satisfied in her craving for a child. Tim, however, could not relent in his abuse of Don Juan. Years more of it followed and only ceased when the police sergeant made his way up to the cottage bearing the last of the thousands of abusive letters which Don Juan's own widow had returned. The last time Mama got out of her bed as a withered, dying nonagenarian was to burn a bundle of letters concerning this affair. She crawled back to bed ready to meet her Lord feeling that she had put the house in order.

Nobody suspected that I was the little boy's father, except Mama and Colette. Meron House was shaken to its solid foundations. Mama had always feared for my 'love of the flesh' more than for her own 'pride of the eyes'. This time I did not laugh at her. My summer days on the Cornish beaches, and rambling over the moors, and mushrooming through dewy meadows had borne an unforseen kind of fruit.

Once again, though shocked, Mama was more wounded. She felt she had failed to protect and guide me. I still resembled Big 'Ina more than Mama. She ought to have done more than instruct Miss Fairweather to give me less meat at the table and never pork. Laura Bell in her open phaeton with her little 'tiger' at the horses' heads among the 'notorious Hetaerae' of Hyde Park had never been so foolish as Mama thought I had been to get myself in such a situation.

For a time, Mama clung to the hope that the letter was just one more piece of mischief. Was it possible that I had succeeded when Don Juan had failed? Poor, rarefied Mama, she had never even allowed Miss Fairweather to write 'toilet rolls' on the weekly grocer's list, but ordered them yearly from a distant chemist.

But Mama had more to charge me with than the evidence of my passions. The world was indeed 'ripe unto harvest'—the harvest of the damned who would not be prepared for the rending of the clouds and the glory of the Lord's return in Mad John Martin fashion. No, I could not deny my passion. And could I deny, demanded Mama, that I was no longer teaching at Clayesmore but was, in fact, acting in the theatre again? What other explanation was there of the fact that she, Mama, had telephoned Clayesmore on three separate occasions only to be told I was not there? Further, Mama had evidence, for I had been seen by some of her friends whilst going about theatrical business.

Unhappy Mama, her image of me as I ought to be, clashed violently with what I was in reality. Yet not all was lost. Her idea that I had deserted Clayesmore for the stage was a fantastic fabrication wrought from a few gossamer threads of misinterpretation. Yes, I *had* been away from the school when she telephoned. Yes, I *had* been seen in the streets of Bath carrying theatrical props. But since I was helping to produce *The Wizard of Oz* at the school, as well as a play in Latin for presentation on parents' day, I had gone to Citizen House in Bath to collect proper costumes. One of her lady friends had seen me walking to the station afterwards carrying some papier mâché Roman helmets on my arm.

What was done could not be undone. Worry and concern for me consumed Mama. The halcyon days were over. But I had become too much part of her life for her to turn me out of the house. She loved me still. But it was plain that I would have to go away, right away for a year or two, until 'the dust settled'.

My first act on hearing about Colette and the child was to telephone and arrange a meeting. Far from being weighted down with sackcloth and ashes, I felt a tremendous excitement and could hardly wait till the week-end when I was to see them both. Our re-union in the clear Cornish air was even more wonderful than I had imagined. Colette had changed, mysteriously but decidedly. Her handsome looks were rosy with a kind of inner health.

We walked as we used to along sea-tidy shore, but her thoughts and talk were constantly of our child. A sad feeling possessed me that something would snatch me away again and that our stroll might be the last. I did not know then that the long train journey from Paddington, the picnic lunch among the rocks was to become an annual event. For a moment, I was grieved to see Colette and the child return down the long shadows of the evening lane to the sea cottage and to Tim with whom she was now happy again. I went back to Clayesmore feeling that I must get away and buy a little farm where I could settle down to a tranquil happiness with Rosemary.

Mama proposed sending me to 'the colonies'. New Zealand was her first choice, since so many of her favourite missionaries came from there. The coloured Christmas cards they sent showing flame trees and exotic tropical flowers excited Mama and she kept the cards up all through the year until new ones arrived the next Christmas. Eventually, however, we compromised and decided on Canada. Was it not, Mama said, ruled by powerful bodies like the Iced Water Baptists who kept practically every province 'dry' and free from the ravages of alcohol? Mama immediately got Aunt Mabel to write to the High Commissioner in London for she had some connection with him.

There seemed to be no other way out of my difficulties. I was desperately disturbed at having to leave Clayesmore. But other things had begun to get on top of me, especially my affairs with the Gurdjieff group. Martin had fastened on me, and was determined either to bend me to his purpose of setting me up as a prophet or to destroy me and mine in the process. Besides, the prospect of a journey to Canada was exciting in itself.

Rosemary was home from Africa and agreed about Canada. I had already been invited some time previously, to stay at a ranch on the Prairies owned by friends of her mother's. Rosemary promised to follow as soon as I had prepared a home for the two of us.

It did not take long to adjust myself to the new circumstances and I looked forward to leaving for Canada. During the last months London had become an embarrassingly small town, a place where my several lives were liable to collide with disastrous results. I lived in constant tension when Rosemary was in London for fear of running into some of the Eaton Square group's less desirable members. Another scandal and quarrel and consequent splintering off from the circle had recently taken place and I did not want Rosemary involved.

Yet avoidance was difficult. Sometimes on a Sunday morning Rosemary and I went to St. Peter's in Eaton Square because it was near the Ladies' Carlton Club. One morning we did meet an actor from Martin's group. I asked him the name of his new play. 'It would really suit you,' he answered with a flick of the wrist, 'it's called *For Love Or Money*.' With that he was gone and I was left to extract whatever nastiness I could from his sarcasm. Was it aimed at my relationship with Rosemary, a voicing of what I knew many people were thinking, that money and title were the attraction and not Rosemary herself? Or was the actor's bomb merely aimed at my performance in Martin's group where it must have been patently obvious that I liked my own position in it more than 'higher learning'? Or, and this is how I liked to interpret his meaning, was it a shrewd guess at how I now regarded Martin, a man whom I despised and feared?

Martin was unscrupulous in his purpose either to make me a tool of his selfish ambition or to ruin me altogether. Because of him my happiness at Meron House was smashed. Because of him the prospects of a bright career in teaching, perhaps for many years at Clayesmore, were wrecked. His hold over me was difficult to break, not simply on account of the vicious letters which now replaced the postcards sent to Meron House, but because he was mad with jealousy and rage against me.

By prevarication I had frustrated his attempts to turn me into a messiah. For years he had been combing the religious underworld for a young man who would play this part in his plans. I was not the first nor the only victim. There was the young Jew called Brian. He was handsome and manly and had a perfect physique. He was an athlete as well as a student of Gurdjieff's 'higher learning'. He married and contrary to expectation, Martin was delighted. But the reason for this only became clear when a son was born to the young couple. Martin wanted to use the baby as an infant oblate in the centre he was trying to set up in the country.

Brian's wife raised objections to Martin's interference and influence in their lives, perhaps realizing what a dangerous man they were involved with. After a violent quarrel, Martin set himself against them. He had not to wait long for the chance of revenge. Financial difficulties began to overwhelm Brian who had no sense of money. In arrears with rent, faced with eviction, and having no other place to take his wife and young son, Brian went to Martin to borrow the necessary small sum. It was less than Martin's expenditure on a normal week's entertainment at Eaton Square. But knowing the distress it would cause, realizing the pain he could inflict, Martin refused. Crushed by his troubles, Brian went away and killed himself.

Martin felt nothing but a sense of achievement. But I was deeply upset. Brian had been my friend, the only one in the group possessed of true innocence. I laid his death at Martin's door and thereafter could think only of the old man as a murderer. At the time I believed it to be a serious possibility that Martin was devising some way to bring about my death also.

After Brian's suicide I hated Martin as I had never hated anybody before. But to break directly and suddenly with him was to court disaster. Private detectives kept constant watch on his victims. He surrounded himself with hired mercenaries whom he blackmailed into performing any dirty work that he wanted done. And he ruled these with an iron hand of fear. Even his domestic servants meant nothing to him. One young man called Philip, whom he kept working for impossible hours on a pittance, took some money from Martin's wallet one day. Without hesitation Martin had him arrested and thought the consequent sentence far too lenient.

From Philip, long before Martin had drawn me fully into his vortex, I learnt about the secrets hidden away in the 'Ark of the Covenant'. This was Martin's name for his writing desk in the library. I had never seen him use it and the roll-top was always kept locked. When Philip told me what was inside I did not believe him. When I saw for myself, however, I was prepared thereafter to believe anything I heard about Martin.

The 'Ark of the Covenant' was revealed to me late one evening when Martin and I had dined out. This in itself was a rare occurrence for Martin disliked food not from his own kitchen.

But his cook had gone off to look after her family in Yorkshire, leaving Martin's stomach to Philip's mercy. By ordinary standards Philip could cook quite well, but not by Martin's. He hated to set cold pheasant and salad before his guests. On the other hand he suffered from a phobia over restaurants, as he also did about hotel dining-rooms and left-over food, public lavatories and being obliged to handle dirty bank-notes.

However, on this particular evening, rather than expose me to the barbarities of Philip's cooking, Martin said we should go to his club. Reinforced with half a bottle of whisky he thought he could face the few soused generals who might also be eating at the club. After the meal we went back to Eaton Square for a nightcap. I drank a lot of brandy and bemused by the warmth in the library and the droning sound of Martin's voice talking cabbalism, I fell asleep in an armchair.

The smell of smoke woke me. I thought the house was on fire. But through the curling fumes I saw Martin standing in his priest's robes and realized that he was burning incense in the room. Martin came towards me, and I saw that with his Church of England robes he was wearing his M.A. hood and silver buckled court shoes. In his hands he bore a cushion on which lay the large family Bible. Martin was dangerously drunk. I looked into his eyes and saw that they were bloodshot and sad. He asked me to read from the Pentateuch which he had missed from having to dine out. With flames leaping up the chimney throwing the room now into crimson gloom, now into grotesque brilliance through the incense murk, now flickering over the fantastic surpliced figure, I read,

And it came to pass, that, when the sun went down, and it was dark, behold a smoking furnace, and a burning lamp that passed between those pieces.

When I looked up from the Bible, Martin had left the room leaving the door ajar and the roll-top of his desk open. Philip's words about the desk came into my mind. I crossed to the 'Ark of the Covenant'. In it lay a tangle of whips and belts, handcuffs and revolvers, and *vergas*—the bull's penis *verga* which until recent times was carried by South American men as a mark of social distinction.

I went into the hall. From somewhere I could hear the thuds, repeated at regular intervals, of whipping. Although Martin's bedroom was out of bounds except when he was ill, I burst into the room. Between the bed and the dressing-table where his wife's hair-brushes were still laid out among the photographs of his children, Martin stood naked and bloody from the wounds of the whip. He hardly seemed to notice me but continued to scourge himself as though possessed. A ring of twisted thorn twigs sat round his head.

He had to be stopped. If he were to kill himself, I should be accused of murder. Under those circumstances, who would believe me innocent? Filled with disgust at the sight, I grabbed Martin's arm and wrenched the whip away. He seemed then to come out of a trance-like unawareness. I told him of my fears, not for him but for myself. He saw reason, and taking off his crown of thorns, he slipped the surplice over his lacerated body like a dressing-gown. We went back to the library again, he barefooted and clinging to me for support.

It was not the brandy of the earlier evening which made me feel sick as we sat talking by the library fire until early next morning. I did not know what rendered me powerless to leave the house, like the rabbit held by the snake on the Russian steppes. Because I had now discovered his secret about the 'Ark of the Covenant' Martin determined that I should know all. Although he was in such a terrible state he went to and fro to his desk and laid each thong, each steel-woven belt, each knotted whip before me. With horror, I watched the bleary-eyed, drunken, old man tottering on his thick varicose-veined legs showing under the blood-stained surplice. Martin tried to explain why he had bought these things. He believed that most had come from Nazi concentration camps and prisons—but only from places where Jews had been massacred.

Martin had acquired part of his collection from a relation of a notorious German commander of an occupied country. By using these instruments on himself Martin imagined he was doing finer spiritual exercises than devout Jews wailing over the ruins of the Temple.

Indulgent though he was even in this spiritual exercise, Martin always stopped short of doing himself any permanent damage. He reserved that for other people, such as Brian, whom he quite cheerfully watched go out of the house to commit suicide.

I was aware of the damage which Martin's influence was doing in my life. Yet the association with him involved such a mixture of feelings and provoked such powerful sentiments that in spite of all my attempts at worldliness and otherworldliness, I could not control myself. A feeling of pity for him ensnared me.

Wealth, social connection, intellectual brilliance, a magnetic personality, none of these things had been able to defend Martin from the worm of tragedy which gnawed away inside him. His wife and his children had forsaken him. And though they might well have had good reasons for doing so, I could only pity Martin's forlornness.

He was a man whose strange nature craved, amongst other things, satisfaction from the warmth and love of a family. Deprivation of this drove him to seek it elsewhere, and always under circumstances and from people who could in no way replace what was lost. Consequently at each new disappointment he became more bitter and vicious than before. To be involved with him and not to pity him was, for me at least, impossible.

During my childhood years in Belfast I had grown accustomed to the suffering inflicted by poverty and by the illness and hunger and desperation brought by poverty. But I was learning now that there was another kind of suffering against which even wealth was impotent, a suffering for which it seemed there was no remedy at all.

I had first come across it in Mama. At times I got terrifying glimpses of pain which went on and on without relief through many years, a long drawn-out torture. Mama had yearned to have grandchildren. Her longing to hear children's voices in the old night-nursery consumed her whole life. And Martin was the same. His younger son, who was nearer Big 'Ina's age than my own, had been his favourite. After years of disappointment over not having grandchildren and natural heirs, Martin did at last have a grandson. But by cruel misfortune the child was a mongol.

Martin could not bring himself to accept these hard blows. He turned in wrath from his family and sought an heir elsewhere. Martin wanted a youth whom he could send to his old school, who would become an undergraduate to impress the Oxford Union by his eloquence as Martin himself had once done.

Everything went wrong. In the end, Martin was reduced to hanging about Marble Arch and looking for eloquence at Speakers' Corner. There, he spoke to anyone with Jewish-looking features or what he thought were Jewish features. As a result he was often beaten up and robbed, but this did not deter him from trying to find Christ in a doss-house or on an Embankment seat.

Although Martin was an object of pity he was also one of terror. I feared him. He had an insane possessiveness not only of things but of people. I did not want to become his property, which I soon sensed would be so. Yet I could not free myself from his extraordinary personal magnetism. Like Senta and the Flying Dutchman, some uncanny inner compulsion made me go after his company, even when, like Senta, I discovered that something diabolical surrounded the man.

The reason for this lay partly in flattery. It flattered me exceedingly to go to Eaton Square. Martin's close circle and his various friends were unlike the usual collection of love- and sex-starved widows and spinsters and religious cranks who gather around people like that. Well-known and eminent men, scientists and writers, went to Martin's house for discussions and meetings about 'higher learning'. It had a profoundly dangerous effect on me when during my own first visit Martin handed me a friend's manuscript which he was correcting, and asked for my opinion of it. I had read and admired the author's books over a long period. To find myself holding his thinly pencilled manuscript and being asked to criticize the work, was flattering in the extreme. To be suddenly thrust into the company of clever men who were Martin's friends gave me a thrill and a pleasure I could not resist, even though it entailed a progressively deeper involvement with Martin.

A further tie with Martin was my sense of religion born in me, I suppose, with my Irish blood. Nobody had so far been able fully to explain or to satisfy this undeniable part of me. In Martin, for all his faults and eccentricities, I fancied I saw glimmerings of what religion really was about.

Through all his life, through all his dabblings with religion, Martin was haunted by the death of Christ. In his last years young Brian's death came to haunt him also, and with more terror and remorse than he ever experienced over the death of Jesus. He could find no peace. 'Higher learning' and the secret amulets of the 'Ark of the Covenant' could not lay the ghost of guiltiness. Gurdjieff's writings could offer him no comfort, nor show him how he could whiten his black soul. The crown of thorns became a burden of despair, the worn-out toy of a worn-out masochist.

In the end Martin abandoned Gurdjieff. As he lay dying in the London Clinic he asked for the Last Sacrament. He was laid out in his often-profaned robes as a priest of the Church of England. And the money intended for the temple of learning in the country eventually went to the foundation of an Oxford prize. I like to think I was partly responsible for this reconciliation with the Church of both our childhood's faith. But by that time my own connection with the Gurdjieff group was long past, as was that with Evan Morgan who similarly abandoned his black magic at death's approach and was mourned with the most fashionable memorial services at Farm Street and Brompton Oratory.

When Martin was dead, it took me many years to sum up his significance in my life. For a long time I hated him, believing that it was solely through him that Mama cut me out of her life and out of her will. But as I grew older, more experienced, and a shade more mature, I relented in my harshness, seeing that perhaps in matters such as these we only reap what we have sown.

CHAPTER XIII

Summer's Farewell

M y future life in Canada began to take shape as plans for departure went ahead. Links were made with various people on the other side of the Atlantic. During prayers on the last morning at Clayesmore the headmaster announced my leaving. It sounded like a knell. The summer term had rushed to its end and everybody was singing 'Lord dismiss us with Thy Blessing'. I felt like Mr. Chips. Then I was on the London-bound school train, forgetful of my gloom for a few hours in the hilarious atmosphere which the Bryanston and Sherbourne boys who were also on the train helped to stir up. With Martin fortunately away in Sussex I could go straight to Paddington and so directly home to Meron House.

I found Mama in a desperate state. The spectre of our great parting shadowed all her doings. Yet she was brave and suggested that we spent the last weeks together quietly so that we might enjoy a time of peace before I left. Although there might be nasty letters in the post, and although Myrtle Dailes might burst on us having escaped once more from her asylum, we tried to forget such things. We lived only for the moments passed among the cotoneaster bowers of Rendezvous Corner, beguiling the slipping hours with Cornish stories livened with verses from *The Jackdaw of Rheims*.

But both Mama and I understood we were only wearing masks modelled to represent a happiness we had once known. The masks mocked us. Through the eye-holes Mama and I regarded each other sadly, aware that the distance between us would inevitably grow greater.

Mama's talk ranged happily enough over the many things we had enjoyed together and the things we had laughed about. But nevertheless a restraint put a brake on completely open conversation. At any moment *he* could crop up, as 'the dear old Vicar' had become to Mama. Over my movements in the house, a similar strain existed. For the first time ever I felt like a visitor instead of one of the family. An absolute ban was still in force on the kitchen. Besides the original business of putting the lady-housekeeper on the shelf, Miss Fairweather was behaving more 'queerly' than ever before.

Mama noticed that whenever I came home now, Miss Fairweather made a 'sight of herself'. Previously her greying locks had only been curled with the tongs ready for Monday's excursion to the chiropodist. But ever since the Jewess from next door had been coming in, the lady-housekeeper's tongs were kept hidden away until I was about.

I pondered this 'queer' behaviour, rather dreading the conclusion that Miss Fairweather must be in love with me. With a lowered voice Mama related how she was woken in the middle of one night feeling as, she put it, 'a presence' in her room. It turned out to be Miss Fairweather who had gone into Mama in a fright because she thought there were rats in her room. And this was not the worst of it. The lady-housekeeper had gone into Mama's room without her dentures, thus turning her usual nervous incoherence into total unintelligibility. There must be something very wrong, Mama thought, for Miss Fairweather to behave in such an agitated and improper way.

In another direction too, Miss Fairweather behaved 'queerly' and out of keeping with her station. The lady-housekeeper had a love of delicate china. Over the years she had collected a number of tea services from her former employers, together with such things as dessert dishes painted by her former governess charges. And now she had sold one valuable set in order to buy me a farewell present. Mama could not understand how Miss Fairweather could so far forget her position as a housekeeper as to buy such an expensive gift for 'the son of the house', particularly as only a few months before she had given me an over-handsome cheque on my birthday.

Even more 'queer' for Mama was the present itself—an electric razor. Mama was shocked. How did an unmarried woman like Miss Fairweather know about such things? Had she gone brazenly into a shop and asked for it? When I informed Mama that some girls also possessed electric razors to shave their legs with, she was outraged once again, and immediately wondered if Miss Fairweather was wasting more electricity in this most modern of wickednesses.

But bigger ripples broke the calm surface of those summer weeks at Meron House. During most of her life Mama had been involved with ships and docks, exporting and importing, chartering and surveying, repairing and launching. Though she lumped all these activities together under the general term 'The Works', she was nevertheless well-versed in the running of shipping exchanges and seamen's pools. But now as we made our slow way to take the air at Rendezvous Corner, the whole shipping life of Britain lay in the stranglehold of a nation-wide strike. Mama was convinced this was the result of putting a Socialist government into power. She feared the strike's consequences. Strikes of any sort were bad enough, but one in which the King had to proclaim a state of emergency sent shivers through her. Her family fortunes had suffered enough from strikes in the 1920's, and now she could see it all happening over again if, indeed, any of us remained alive. The Archbishop of Canterbury was talking about a direct threat to national security. And Mama listened intently to this, in spite of being on the point of writing to the Archbishop for talking Tory propaganda when he said 'political good sense is good Christianity too'.

Mama was not only concerned for the Curry-Gowan fortunes, but also for me. The strikes started over some Canadian seamen. Every day we read about world boycott of Canadian ships, or about Canadian crews going to jail or about others being beaten up. And I was on the eve of going to Canada! It was not surprising that Aunt Mabel had received no answer from Canada House for it had been stormed by rebel seamen. Mama began to think that New Zealand would have been better after all. It was farther away from the United States for one thing and for another the world's finest missionary nurses came from there.

But the doom foreseen by the Archbishop and dreaded by Mama gave Britain a miss and before I was due to leave the troops stopped unloading butter and lamb and the strikes were over. Detailed arrangements for my journey had now to be made. Remembering my wide-eyed wanderings as a boy along Belfast's docks, where sailing ships on the Australian grain-races began, I wanted now to travel on the *Aquitania*, 'The Queen of the Ocean', for she would soon be scrapped. Mama's normal cheerfulness did not return fully when the strike ended, for the newspapers still devoted a lot of space to the rebel Canadian seamen being repatriated or put into prison.

However, when a letter came for me from Montreal, Mama brightened and even became excited about Canada. The letter was from my father's sister. Unlike so many of my relatives, my aunt was 'saved'. She used scriptural notepaper and Gospel seals. This greatly impressed Mama. Obviously, the Lord was opening this Christian home in direct answer to prayer, and without delay a cable went off to the Plymouth Brethren household in Montreal.

What I did not tell Mama was that nearly twenty years earlier my aunt and uncle had caused as much controversy as the Canadian strikers of 1949. They had been suspects in the Lindbergh kidnapping. Angry crowds had stormed their little house for many days because my young cousin bore a striking resemblance to Charles Augustus Lindbergh, the missing baby.

Then, all at once it seemed, time had run out. Sea-asters were indeed summer's farewell to the saltings and cliffs. These blue-purple daisies were the last flowers Mama and I ever picked together. And more sadly, our walks together on those few remaining days were to be the last she ever took, for although she lived through another decade they were unhappy,

Summer's Farewell

bed-ridden years with Roberto's ghost around every corner.
Dearest, kindest, most bigoted little Mama used her pen for the
last time in writing to me 'Yours is one of those faces I have
loved and lost awhile, but I pray not eternally.'

While watching my trunk being tied on the car for the drive
to Southampton where the *Aquitania* lay, Mama tried not to
show her emotions as Miss Fairweather was doing. Mama gave
me the address of a Christian boarding-house in Southampton
where I should spend the night before joining the ship next
day. Then she gave me her special kiss on the forehead,
accompanied by a sharp glance at Miss Fairweather which told
her not to make a fool of herself. Then the little, old woman
went back into the empty, silent house to wait and pray, to wait
for my first letter from Canada, and to pray on through the
remaining years that I might be given the whole armour of
God. The helmet of salvation I undoubtedly possessed. But
was my sword made quick by the Spirit, would my shield be
able to quench all the fiery darts of Canada's wickedness, were
my loins girded about with truth?

But, of course, Mama was right in knowing that even now
my spiritual armour was not as bright as she hoped. How could
I tell her that the note of departure I was writing was not being
written in the Christian boarding-house, but in a rowdy
Southampton dock-side café full of Canadian seamen who were
being repatriated on the *Aquitania*, noisy, couldn't-care-less
youngsters who were to be my constant companions on the
voyage? Mama would have sorely grieved if she had seen the
crisp new notes, fetched from the bank by Miss Fairweather
for my expenses, being sent off to Big 'Ina in Belfast. The tears
she held back yesterday at our parting would have flowed full
had she seen me write a farewell note to Colette.

The boisterous bravado, the thunderous pulse of young
blood aboard ship was so very different from the quiet, pale
life of Meron House. I felt terrified that any of the seamen
should guess what kind of life I had just left. Mama had cut
roses and jasmine from the garden and given them to me,
thinking they would be a last breath of Meron House in my

cabin, enough to carry me across the Atlantic. But I had no cabin, for the *Aquitania* was still unconverted from its war-time service as a troop-ship.

My berth was supposed to have been in a cabin with four-teen British people emigrating to Canada. But they were dull and respectable and not at all what I wanted by way of com-pany for my first trans-Atlantic crossing. So as soon as I dis-covered a vacant bunk in one of the Canadian seamen's dormi-tories, I moved in with them.

Poor Mama's roses, they could not be put on show among the festoons of jockey pants hung up to dry between the bunks. Neither would a whole hedge of jasmine have sweetened the cigarette-clogged air. Mama would have swooned in horror at the sight of thirty young men strutting naked between the cabin and shower-baths, flicking towels at each other's buttocks. Miss Fairweather would have felt very queer indeed to see the drunken young sailors using the wash-basins instead of the proper Certain Articles.

And if Mama thought it improper for me to have seen her lady-housekeeper's legs dangling from the high kitchen shelf, what would she have said about the huge, hairy thighs swing-ing contentedly over the edge of bunks? The staircase of Meron House was enlivened by Mad John Martin's resurrec-tion orgies, but what would its owner have thought of the muscular bodies that wrestled and writhed, panting and sweating, no holds barred, on the cabin floor?

Mama, who loved the peace of Rendezvous Corner, would have been driven mad by the noise, the singing and shouting. She would have understood nothing of the seamen's back-chat about clap and blue boils, Spanish fly and Maltese jack. Mama could never have believed that this was her beloved Roberto. Forty-eight hours earlier he had been singing evangelical praises from *Chants de Gloire et de Victoire*. Now he was shout-ing with the throaty, fruity Canadian seamen:

> *The sailors they ride in a row-boat,*
> *The captain he rides in a barge,*

Summer's Farewell

Not that he gets there any faster,
But it gives the old bugger a charge.

Because she saw none of this, Mama's tears were spared. And this was well. For although I would never wear my black preaching clothes again, and had forever forsaken my Anthony Eden hat and sermon note-books, I could never forsake the love and kindness which surrounded me during those four years at Meron House. Whatever the future held, there would be no escape from the hours when Mama tried to give me Latin and music, and all the airs and graces of a Victorian gentleman.

Patiently, lovingly, Mama had gathered up the fragments of my earlier life, fashioning them into what she hoped was a vessel meet for the Lord's use. Neither Mama nor I knew then how many times the vessel was to be cracked in the years that still lay ahead. But the future did not worry me. I slept soundly enough as we pitched and rolled across the Atlantic where Mama's own ships had ploughed to bring the fortunes of Meron House.